I0482648

Communication
Skill Builders

20 Icebreakers & Training Activities

by

Louis E. Tagliaferri, Ph.D.

Ponte Vedra, Florida 32082
904-285-7757
www.talico.com

Published by Louis E. Tagliaferri
Ponte Vedra Beach, Florida 32082
Printed in the United States of America

Copyright Louis E. Tagliaferri 2000-2014

Reproduction Notice

This volume is a compendium, and all chapters, sections and appendixes thereto, are the copyrighted work of the author and are the proprietary product of the author and publisher. All rights are reserved. The purchase of this volume includes a limited site license for the purchaser to reproduce, through photocopy or other means, and use the student material contained herein among its own employees, or, if the purchaser is a consultant, among the employees of one (1) of its clients for educational purposes. However, modification of the material in any manner, in whole or in part, including but not limited to the deletion of the copyright notice, logos, author's name or the incorporation of this product in other works, or resale of the product, without the express permission of the author is strictly prohibited.

ISBN-13: 978-1496093394
ISBN-10: 1496093399

Dedicated to the thousands of employees in business, industry and government who have improved their communication skills as a result of participating in the training activities presented in this book.

Table of Contents

Introduction

Welcome to *Communication Skill Builders: 20 Icebreakers & Training Activities*, a series of activities, exercises and role plays that range from icebreakers and energizers to activities that can serve as the foundation for a more extensive communication training module. Even better, all of the activities, exercises and role plays in this volume together comprise the requisites you need to construct a complete communication skills training program. The icebreakers and training activities are fun for participants, easy for you to administer, powerful enough to really motivate yet short enough so that the activities do not interfere with the main objectives of your training session. Equally important, *Communication Skill Builders: 20 Icebreakers & Training Activities* have excellent technical content and each activity makes its point clearly and dramatically -- experiential learning at its best!

This volume begins with a section titled **Tips for Trainers**. It is an important section which you should read before using any of the exercises because it contains useful suggestions that will help you prepare your training session more effectively. The section includes a standard introductory format that is applicable to all of the activities and exercises.

Each activity begins with a synopsis which is a general overview of the activity's objective, its description and that contains other important general information. This is followed by the **Key Principles** section which contains all of the background information that most trainers will need to present the activity. If you need reinforcement about any of the relevant principles in the subject areas covered by this volume <u>be sure</u> that you take the time before class to research the subject more fully by reading any of the many publically available works about communication, its attributes and elements. Do not be caught unprepared!

The **Facilitation Guidelines** for the activity are step-by-step suggestions that you can follow to ensure that the activity is presented in the most effective way. However, experienced platform presenters should feel free to modify these guidelines so that they are consistent with presentation method with which the presenter is most comfortable. Lastly, several useful observer checklists are included in an **Appendix** section that will be found following the activity section.

Note: The terms "activities" and "exercises" are used interchangeably in this work.

Tips for Trainers

The purpose of this section is to give you some guidelines and suggestions that can make facilitating the activities in this series even easier. You can begin by reading this section thoroughly. Remember, your effectiveness as a facilitator will in large part determine the success of your program. Here are some tips that will help to make your job easier:

1. **Commitment**

    The first step in the preparation phase is to ensure that you have the commitment of top management for your training. Management must set the stage by emphatically and enthusiastically expressing its position that the training program is both needed and desirable.
    Without this endorsement, acceptance and cooperation at lower levels may be only half-hearted.

2. **Time**

    Each of the activities in this series is designed to be presented in from 15 to 30 minutes. You can extend the time of each exercise as you may choose by adding other Talico Inc. material or other material that you might design. Also, you can control the amount of time that you choose to allocate to an exercise by determining how much time you want to devote to introduce the exercise and how much debriefing time you want.

3. **Physical Arrangements**

    a. <u>Where to hold the Training Meeting</u> - Holding training meetings in-house saves money and travel time. On the other hand, being in the plant or office can result in disruptions, such as people being called out to answer the phone or handle problems. Also consider whether in-house facilities are conducive to learning; for example, are they clean, neat, and comfortable? Can the facility supply the audio/visual equipment that you will need? If not, you may want to arrange for course sessions to be held in other facilities. Motels or hotels often have comfortable meeting rooms which can be rented at nominal cost. Your area may have other suitable facilities, as well.

b. <u>The Meeting Room</u> - Wherever you hold the training meeting, you will want to ensure that the room itself is suitable; large enough to accommodate everyone comfortably, well ventilated, heated or air conditioned, and well lit. Also, be sure that the room is located where it is free from distracting noise.

c. <u>Room Arrangement</u> - You will need tables and chairs for all participants and for the instructor. If you plan to have the participants work on problems in teams, arrange for separate tables for each team. You also will need a table for refreshments, if you provide them.

d. <u>Equipment and Supplies</u> - Be sure to have the required resource material, including pencils and paper for each participant, available for the training session. You may benefit by making overhead transparencies of key learning points developed in your sessions; in which case an overhead projector will also be needed. Also, a flip chart or chalkboard is useful for most sessions.

4. Methods of Instruction

The following alternative presentation methods are discussed for your general interest. It is possible to combine several methods in one session.

a. <u>Lecture</u> - A very common teaching method, this involves the instructor making a one-way presentation to the group. Its advantage is that it involves a high amount of control over the communication process since communication is primarily in one direction, downward.

However one way communication also has certain disadvantages; you receive little, if any, feedback from the group and the process by its nature is non-participative. If you do lecture, do so sparingly. A lecture can be a boring method from the group's perspective.

b. Lecturette - This is similar to a lecture but very brief, usually 5-10 minutes in duration. A lecturette can be most effective when used in conjunction with other methods.

c. Group Discussion - This is a very good instructional method for actively involving the class. The leader functions primarily as a catalyst by introducing the subject, using questions to ensure group participation, keeping the discussion on track and, periodically, summarizing and testing for the group's conclusions. Group discussion in conjunction with lecturettes can be an effective mix of teaching methods.

d. Role Playing - Role playing is a proven method by which a person practices a skill he or she is learning. In role playing, each person is assigned a role (either prepared roles or ones that they write themselves) which describes a problem situation and provides information about the character to be played, all relating to the subject of the lesson. Usually two students role play together, one taking the role of an employee and the other that of a supervisor.

The role play participants act out the situation under the observation of their fellow participants. At the conclusion of the brief skit (usually 5-10 minutes), all parties critique the skills demonstrated.

Role playing is especially helpful when the demonstration of a skill will enhance the learning process. Performance appraisal and employee counseling skills are examples of subjects suitable for role playing.

e. Team Activity - This method is very useful when you want the participants to work together cooperatively to make a decision or solve a problem. First, you should divide the class into teams of from 4 to 6 people each, and seat each team at a separate table. You then assign problems or situations to each team and let them collectively discuss, analyze, and solve it.

Next, ask each team to appoint a spokesperson who reports the team's finding and discusses the problem solving or decision making process. This is followed by the rest of the group critiquing the team's work.

There is some question about the optimum size group for this type of activity. As a rule of thumb you should not have teams of less than 4 people each <u>unless</u> you intentionally are setting up diads or triads (teams of two or three, respectively). Teams of less than 4 people are very easily dominated by only 1 or 2 people.

On the other hand, the maximum number of individuals on a team should be less than 10 or 12. Teams larger than this very often result in poor participation by several team members; the team is simply to cumbersome to actively involve all of the members.

5.   **Standard Introduction**

Each activity begins with a brief synopsis that is designed to provide you with a quick overview of the activity. This is followed by **Key Principles** that provide important background concepts and then a **Facilitation Guidelines** section which offers suggestions for administering the exercise effectively. If you are an experienced platform trainer or facilitator you may choose to tailor the presentation to your personal instructional style. If facilitating exercises like these is new to you then you will probably benefit by following the facilitation guidelines closely.

In any event, there is a standard way that you can begin each session. Because of this, and to avoid redundancy, we are including the guidelines for that standard introduction among these **Tips for Trainers**.

a.   Read the entire exercise, including all exhibits, thoroughly. Make certain that you understand the learning principles that you want developed by administering the exercise and that you also understand any related technical concept. If you are not entirely clear about these principles you should refer to the many articles and texts about the subject which are readily available at public and company libraries.

b. Begin the exercise session by explaining the purpose of the exercise and the specific learning objectives that you have determined for the group. Present a brief overview of the exercise concept; but be careful not to give away details that might be reserved for only part of the group.

c. Relate the exercise with the overall training module that you are conducting and explain its part in the learning process. Explain what is meant by experiential learning and tell the group how gaming simulations and role plays facilitate learning. This is necessary because sometimes students find it curious that a "game" is being made part of an instructional program.

d. If you are facilitating a session for a large group you may want to appoint one or two co-facilitators who will help you observe and record individual and team behavior during the exercise.

e. Sometimes a good strategy for using an exercise is to begin without any explanation, administer the exercise, and then after experiential learning has taken place cover the issues in numbers "b" and "c" above. This "shock treatment" approach can be very useful when you want to dramatize certain points.

```
┌─────────────────────────────┐
│                             │
│       Activity No. 1        │
│       Why We Do It          │
│                             │
└─────────────────────────────┘
```

Time: About 45 to 50 minutes

Purpose: The objective of this activity is to familiarize students with the
                     major purposes and uses of communication.

Description: Teams of employees are assigned to brainstorm as many reasons
                     as they can for communication among people. They then
                     categorize their lists into major purposes or objectives of
                     communication and prepare short examples that illustrate the
                     distinguishing characteristics of each type of communication. The
                     teams share their findings with all members of the class as the
                     facilitator leads a group discussion about the subject and relates
                     team findings to the work environment of the organization.

Material/Props: Note pads with pencils or pens for the teams, flip charts with
                     paper, markers and masking tape.

Teams/Group: Teams of four to six people each with a maximum of 25 people in
                     the class. Additional facilitators will be required for larger classes
                     not to exceed 40 people in total.

Application: Suitable for employees at all organizational levels.

There are few human behaviors that are taken for granted as much and as often as communication. In most cases people simply exchange messages with each other spontaneously without giving a great deal of thought to the reason why they are communicating. They have a thought that they want to get across to someone else and they simply do so – almost unconsciously formatting the thought into a message and likewise choosing the method, channel or media by which the message will be conveyed.

However random the process may at times seem, there are several very distinct reasons why people communicate. These are referred to as the purposes of communication. Among them are the following:

1. *To inform:* This purpose is the essence of communication. It is one of the main reasons why we exchange messages with each other. We share information about all those things that we consider important as well as all those which may be trivial. An essential component of information sharing is feedback. When we share information the quality of communication is enhanced by any feedback that we receive from the other person. This applies to all purposes of communication.

2. *To educate:* When we communicate with the intent of educating (or of training) we also share information. But in this case we are not simply informing someone or a class or a group of people about something. Instead we are imparting knowledge and in the feedback process we want to make sure that the message receiver both understands and has learned from what we communicated. This purpose stretches from the primary school classroom to graduate seminars and to on-the-job skills training sessions for employees.

3. *To persuade:* This purpose may include an intent to both inform and to educate but it is distinctly different fro either. We can inform and even educate without trying to persuade people to accept our line of reasoning. For example, people can be informed about a certain organization policy without being persuaded that it is useful or fair. They can be taught certain work methods but they may not believe that those methods are efficient. But, when we communicate to persuade, our intent is to convert another person or a group of people to our line of thinking or to

endorse a position that we espouse or to a similar end. Presidential political debates, for example, are designed exactly for that purpose. Likewise, advertising campaigns are designed to persuade consumers to purchase certain products.

4. *To entertain:* People communicate just to have fun. Most of us tell jokes, tell or listen to stories, watch movies and TV, enjoy various forms of art, and otherwise use communication to provide or receive entertainment of one kind or another. Music, by the way, for those who write musical compositions, play musical instruments and who just enjoy listening to it, is most definitely a form of communication.

5. *To socialize:* Certainly a core purpose of communication is to establish and maintain social relationships with others. Affiliation or human social interaction is one of the most basic human needs. From a practical perspective it is essentially impossible for human interaction to exist without communication taking place, whether verbal or nonverbal.

There are many other purposes of communication. Many are subsets of the five listed above. For example, purposes for communicating with others could include: to counsel employees, to promote healing , to facilitate technological advancement or for spiritual reasons. All of these and others may be valid purposes of communication which this activity will help your class identify.

The purpose of this section is to help you facilitate the activity effectively. Before administering the activity to your class or session participants be sure to read it in its entirety. If there are any aspects of the Key Principles about which you are unclear we suggest that you review the subject by referring to one or more of the many reference works which are readily available at any public library and at most company libraries.

1.   Introduce the activity by asking the class why they communicate with others. Choose a few responses from the class and list them on a flip chart but do not discuss them at this time. State the purpose and objective of the activity and tell the class that when they have completed it they will have a much better understanding about the purposes of communication.

2.   Divide the class into teams of from four to six people each. Make sure that each team is comfortably seated together and that they have the required material or props.

3.   Instruct the teams to brainstorm a list of reasons why people communicate with each other. Be sure to remind them that brainstorm lists should be confined to one to three words per idea and that all ideas are welcome, i.e. no judgement of anyone's ideas at this point. Allow about five to 10 minutes for this task.

4.   At the end of five to 10 minutes halt the brainstorm exercise. Inform the teams that their next task is to "clean up" their lists by eliminating duplicates and inappropriate items. Then, tell them that they are to develop at least five categories of communication purposes and to allocate the individual communication reasons or purposes in their lists among those categories. Allow them to develop and name whatever categories they want. Allow 10 minutes for this part of the activity.

5.   After 10 minutes distribute sheets of flip chart paper along with masking tape. Tell the class to write the categories (including the subset of reasons or

10

purposes within each category) on the flip chart paper and post it on a wall in the class room. Also tell the teams to select a spokesperson for their team. Allow five minutes for this task.

6.   After five minutes halt the activity and have the spokesperson from each team present the team's findings. Briefly discuss the differences and similarities among the various lists (most differences will be semantic). However, focus the main thrust of the discussion on why it is important to understand that there are distinctly different reasons why people communicate with each other. Include in the discussion how the nature, form and method of communication will likely vary with each different purpose. Have the class develop and discuss specific illustrations about this and relate them to the work environment within your organization.

7.   After about 15 minutes bring the discussion to a close. Ask for and answer any final questions and then adjourn the session.

```
┌─────────────────────────────────┐
│         Activity No.  2         │
│         How It Works            │
└─────────────────────────────────┘
```

Time: About 40 to 45 minutes

Purpose: The objective of this activity is to familiarize students with the
                   process of communication.

Description: Students are shown a two-way communication model, which is
                   explained by the facilitator. Volunteers from the class take the
                   roles of message senders, message receivers and message blockers.
                   Message senders then attempt to communicate with message
                   receivers in a way that overcomes barriers set up by the message
                   blockers.

Material/Props: Note pads with pencils or pens, flip charts with paper and
                   marker, one copy of **Handout 2.1** for all participants and one
                   copy of **Handouts 2.2, 2.3, 2.4** and **2.5** for the role play
                   participants as suggested in the **Facilitation Guidelines**. You
                   will also need either a radio or cassette player with a loud,
                   raucous music tape.

Teams/Group: This activity is designed to be administered to the class as a whole.
                   However, at the facilitator's option it can be administered as a
                   team activity by dividing the class into teams of from 8 to 10
                   students each.

Application: Most suitable for employees at lower and middle organizational
                   levels.

Key Principles

In order for communication as we know it to exist there must be a minimum of three elements:

1. **Message**. Basically, this is a thought. The thought, or message, must be put into a form that can be sent to someone. The form can be oral, written, digital, pictorial, graphic or some other form that will be understood by another person.

2. **Sender**. This is the person who has the thought or message to be sent to someone else.

3. **Receiver**. Obviously, this is the person who gets the message that is sent by the message sender.

The sender has a message that he or she wants to send to someone else, the receiver. The first challenge is that the sender must take the thought, which is the basis of the message, and encode it or put it into a form in which it can be transmitted to the receiver. The sender immediately encounters all kinds of problems as he or she begins this process. For example, there may be language and semantic problems. The sender must make sure that the message is accurate, that what is communicated is what the sender meant to say. The message must be directed to the correct audience or receiver and methods of transmitting the message must be selected.

The process is no easier for the receiver. There are many barriers through which the message must pass before it reaches the receiver. The receiver must decode the message through his or her own screen of barriers, like preconception, prejudice, culture, personality, distraction, and a lot more before communication can be completed. Then, in order to close the communication loop, the receiver must respond to the message in some way. This usually involves the receiver becoming a sender of a return message, feedback, and the process repeats itself in reverse.

The purpose of this section is to help you facilitate the activity effectively. Before administering the activity to your class or session participants, be sure to read it in its entirety. If there are any aspects of the Key Principles about which you are unclear we suggest that you review the subject by referring to one or more of the many reference works which are readily available at any public library and at most company libraries.

1. Introduce the activity by distributing one copy of **Handout 2.1** to all members of the class. Present a brief explanation of the Two-Way Model of Communication in the handout, using the information in **Key Principles** above as a guideline. Be sure to include and discuss examples of the elements of encoding, decoding and the potential message blockers of environment, personality and perception screens.

2. Ask for volunteers from the class to take the roles of message sender, message receiver, and message blockers. There should be one message blocker each for the message sender and message receiver (a total of two blockers). Separate the message sender and his or her blocker from the message receiver and his or her blocker by a sufficient space within the class room (but still at the front of the class) so that any conversation between them and their respective message blocker cannot be easily overheard by the other party. Provide note paper and writing instruments to both sets of parties.

3. Distribute one copy of **Handout 2.2** to the person who role plays the message sender, one copy of **Handout 2.3** to the person who role plays the message receiver , one copy of **Handout 2.4** to the person who role plays   the blocker for the message sender and one copy of **Handout 2.5** for the person who role plays the blocker for the message receiver. Ask them to read their respective roles and answer any questions that they might have **in private** so that neither the class nor other role players can overhear either the role player's question or your answer.

4. Tell the class that the purpose of this activity is to demonstrate the process of communication and to explain why sometimes it is difficult for messages to be conveyed from one person to another accurately and effectively. Refer again to the model in **Handout 2.1**. Review the roles of the volunteers and state that the job of each message blocker is to try to add an influence that will inhibit the real intent and purpose of the message that is being exchanged between the two parties. Ask the class to make notes about what they observe during the activity and to be prepared to discuss their observations during the activity debriefing.

5. Tell the role players to begin the activity and inform them that they will have no more than 25 minutes to complete it. Then turn on the radio or cassette player to a volume loud enough that it could be somewhat of a distraction to the role players but not loud enough to be obnoxious to the whole class. The purpose of playing the radio or cassette player is to simulate environmental noise and distraction.

6. Allow the activity to proceed until the message cycle is complete but no longer than 25 minutes, unless you decide to extend the time at your option. Then halt the activity, turn off the radio or cassette player and begin a debriefing.

7. Ask the message sender to tell the class what his or her message assignment was. Have that person tell the class to what extent encoding was affected by the information added by that person's message blocker and by the simulated environmental noise and distraction. Next, ask the message receiver to what extent his or her decoding of the sender's message and response (feedback) was affected by information added by that person's message blocker. Conclude by asking the original message sender to what extent his or her interpretation of the response (feedback) from the message receiver was affected by perception or other barriers. Now direct the discussion to the class as a whole for a few minutes to obtain their opinions about the process which they observed.

8. After about 10 minutes bring the discussion to a close. Ask for and answer any final questions and then adjourn the session.

Figure 2.1   **Two-Way Communication Model**

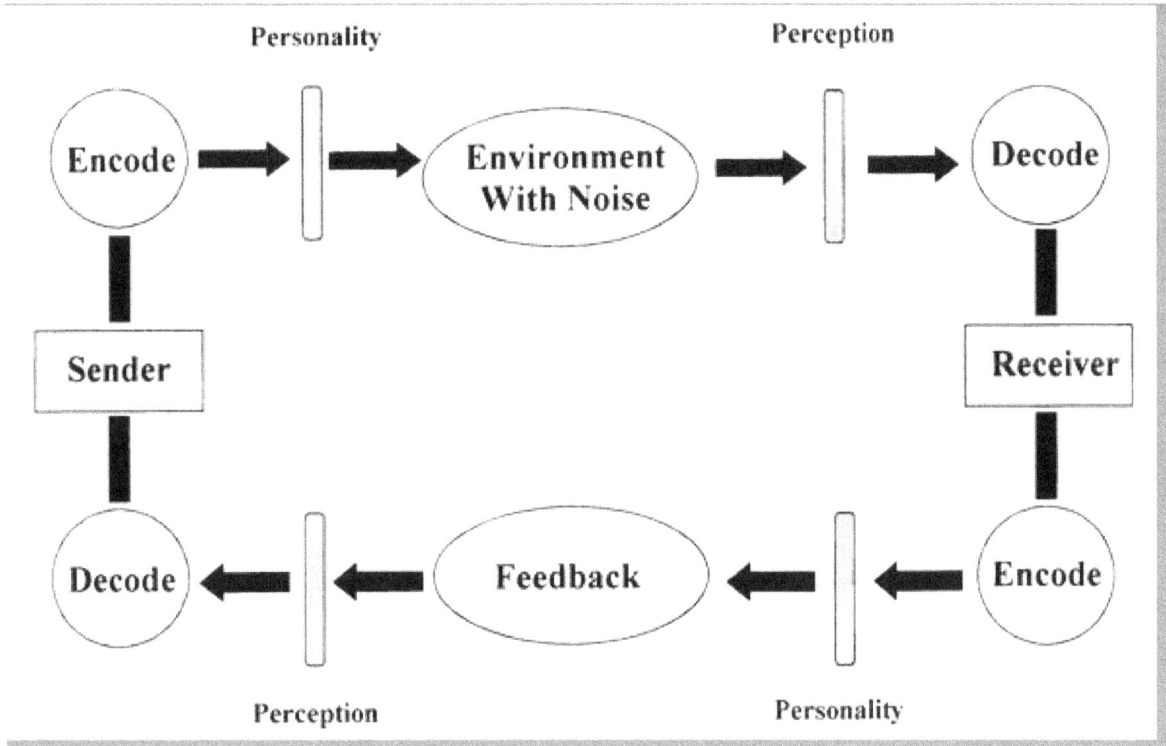

Handout 2.2   **Instructions for Message Sender**

You are the manager of financial services in a 300 employee healthcare organization. Part of your responsibility includes the preparation of the organization's annual operating budget. In the past there have been difficulties with forecasting accuracy on the part of certain departments. So, this year you are preparing a personal memo to be sent to each department head to help ensure that their budget forecasts are accurate and consistent with the financial guidelines of your organization.

In this particular case you are writing the memo to the person who is the department head of purchasing. You are to write a memo that does not exceed 50 words and you will have 10 minutes to do so. When the memo is completed pass it on to the person who is role playing the message receiver.

Handout 2.3   **Instructions for Message Receiver**

You are the manager of purchasing in a 300 employee healthcare organization. It is annual budget preparation time and you will soon be asked to prepare your department's budget forecast for the next fiscal year. In a few minutes a request for the budget will be sent to you in the form of a memo. Although you have one month to prepare the budget you will be asked to respond to the memo now. When you receive it prepare a response that does not exceed 50 words and pass it on to the person who gave it to you, the message sender. You will have 10 minutes to make your response.

Handout 2.4   Instructions for Message Sender's Blocker

The scenario is a 300 employee healthcare organization where the message sender is the manager of financial services and the message receiver is the department head responsible for purchasing. It is the time to prepare the annual operating budget. Last year budget forecasts from the various department heads were inaccurate and caused considerable trouble as actual expenses and costs exceeded those which were forecast. This year the message sender is sending a personal memo to each department head, including the message receiver, in which he or she will try to ensure that budget forecasts for the next fiscal year are more accurate than in the past.

The message sender and the message receiver have had a personal conflict for several years. The message sender is convinced that the message receiver deliberately puffs up budget requests to ensure that there is extra money available for whatever he or she wants to spend during the year and still end the year apparently under budget. In other words, asking for more than is needed and then spending most but not all of it, thus giving a false impression of fiscal responsibility.

As the blocker for the message sender you are to use the information in this handout to influence his or her preparation of the memo.

Handout 2.5   Instructions for Message Receiver's Blocker

The scenario is a 300 employee healthcare organization where the message sender is the manager of financial services and the message receiver is the department head responsible for purchasing. It is the time to prepare the annual operating budget. Last year budget forecasts from the various department heads were inaccurate and caused considerable trouble as actual expenses and costs exceeded those which were forecast. This year the message sender is sending a personal memo to each department head, including the message receiver, in which he or she will try to ensure that budget forecasts for the next fiscal year are more accurate than in the past.

The message receiver believes that he or she has done very well with respect to annual budget forecasts and that his or her department should be commended because it consistently ends the year spending less than budgeted, thus saving money for the organization. The message receiver is a very proud person and would resent any suggestion of impropriety in budget preparation.

As the blocker for the message receiver you are to use the information in this handout to influence his or her perception of the sender's message and also you are to influence his or her response to the message sender.

Activity No. 3
Caution! Pitfalls Ahead

Time: About 45 to 50 minutes

Purpose: The objective of this activity is to familiarize students with some of the more common pitfalls that can adversely affect the quality of interpersonal communication.

Description: Teams of employees are assigned to use the brainstorming technique to compile a list of the most common types of communication pitfalls that adversely affect the quality of interpersonal communication within their organization on a day-to-day basis. They then select the top three pitfalls affecting their work teams and develop practical ways to avoid them in the future. The teams share their findings with all members of the class as the facilitator leads a group discussion about the subject and relates team findings to the total work environment of the organization.

Material/Props: Note pad with pencils or pens for the teams, flip charts with paper, markers and masking tape.

Teams/Group: Teams of four to six people each with a maximum of 25 people in the class. Additional facilitators will be required for larger classes not to exceed 40 people in total.

Application: Suitable for employees at all organizational levels.

Key Principles

Many years ago communication expert Mickey Dover said that communication within organizations was a billion dollar bungle. What he was referring to was the amount of time and money that is wasted within organizations by poor communication practices. Some of this waste is fairly easy to visualize. It is obvious, for example, that time is wasted and money is lost when a misunderstood order results in a retail catalog company shipping the wrong product to a customer or when poorly communicated work instructions results in a job being done incorrectly. But, communication is perhaps the most pervasive human interaction in any organization and sometimes the effects of poor communication are more subtle.

Consider the problem of lack of teamwork among interdependent work units. In that type of situation a communication problem may be more covert – like one work unit simply not fully sharing information that is important to the effective functioning of another work unit. That could cause many kinds of problems in the latter work unit such as redundant work effort, under or over production of a product or service, quality problems and much more. Often, problems like these extend beyond only a few work units and can stretch to the entire organization or even to people outside the organization like customers, vendors and even stockholders. For instance, recently the senior management of one major company in the technology industry allegedly intentionally withheld "bad news" about sales and profits in order to keep the market value of the corporations stock high. When the truth was revealed the stock plummeted and shareholders lost billions of dollars.

While it may not be possible to imagine every possible type of communication problem that can occur in an organization or within a work unit, it is possible to identify the most common communication pitfalls. If one believes in the "80/20" rule then by identifying and avoiding the most common 20% of communication pitfalls, it is possible to eliminate or minimize 80% of all communication related problems.

So, exactly what are these major communication pitfalls? Well, in part that is what this exercise is designed to help your students determine – at least as they apply to work related conditions and efficiencies within your organization. During this activity you will be asking the class to identify communication problems that may be preventing them and the other members of their work units from being as effective as they would like to be in their jobs. The chances are that while many of these pitfalls are common to all organizations, some may be very particular to yours. In any event, by the time that the activity is concluded your teams will likely have identified some of the following communication pitfalls (illustrative list only):

- Failure to listen effectively
- Carelessness or distraction
- Preoccupation with personal or business problems
- Failure to accurately define a problem or decision issue
- Imprecise definition of the message
- Language or semantic problems
- Bias or prejudice
- Failure to share information with those who need it
- Time pressures
- Information overload
- Interpersonal conflict or unproductive competition
- Lack of training in communication methods
- Improper use of communication channels or media
- Lack of communication feedback
- Failure to use communication aids like charts or pictures.
- Poor meeting or conference leadership
- Lack of teamwork
- Lack of attention to "body language"
- Improper use of jargon or local terminology
- Poor writing skills

A short activity like this will not be able to solve all of your organization's communication problems. But it can begin the process by making class participants more aware about the kinds of communication pitfalls that affect them daily and by focusing their attention on the top few pitfalls that when avoided or eliminated will help them become more effective communicators!

The purpose of this section is to help you facilitate the activity effectively. Before administering the activity to your class or session participants be sure to read it in its entirety. If there are any aspects of the Key Principles about which you are unclear we suggest that you review the subject by referring to one or more of the many reference works which are readily available at any public library and at most company libraries.3

1.   Introduce the activity by asking the class what kind of problems most seriously affect them on their jobs. Choose a few responses from the class and list the examples on a flip chart. Check those that are clearly communication related. State the purpose and objective of the activity and tell the class that when they have completed it they will have a greater awareness about how communication pitfalls can adversely affect their work and how to avoid the most serious pitfalls.

2.   Divide the class into teams of from four to six people each. Make sure that each team is comfortably seated together and that they have the required material or props.

3.   Instruct the teams to brainstorm a list of communication pitfalls that they regularly encounter on the job. Be sure to remind them that brainstorm lists should be confined to one to three words per idea and that all ideas are welcome, i.e. no judgement of anyone's ideas at this point. Allow about five to 10 minutes for this task.

4.   At the end of five to 10 minutes halt the brainstorm exercise. Then, tell the teams that they are to select the three communication pitfalls from among those that they have listed that have the greatest negative affect on themselves and the other members of their work unit. Tell them that when they have identified the three they are then to develop at least one practical way by which each of the three pitfalls can be avoided in the future. Allow 20 minutes for this part of the activity.

5.   After 20 minutes distribute sheets of flip chart paper along with masking tape. Tell the class to write the three selected communication pitfalls and their solutions for avoiding or eliminating each on flip chart paper and to post the paper on a wall in the class room. Also tell the teams to select a spokesperson for their team. Allow five minutes for this task.

6.   After five minutes halt the activity.   Briefly discuss the differences and similarities among the various lists. Then have the spokesperson from each team present his or her team's findings.   Be sure to ask each spokesperson in what particular way the three pitfalls have adversely affected them and what the specific beneficial effect will be if the pitfalls can be avoided or eliminated.

7.   After about 15 minutes bring the discussion to a close. Ask for and answer any final questions and then adjourn the session.

Activity No. 4
Messenger Service

Time: About 25 to 30 minutes

Purpose: The objective of this activity is to familiarize students with the many ways by which messages of any type can be transmitted from one place to another or from one person to another.

Description: Teams of students brainstorm lists of message transmission methods and decide what kind of message is most effectively transmitted by each method that they identified.

Material/Props: Note pads with pencils or pens, flip charts with paper and markers, masking tape.

Teams/Group: Teams of four to six people each with a maximum of 25 people in the class. Additional facilitators will be required for larger classes not to exceed 40 people in total.

Application: Most suitable for employees at lower and middle organizational levels.

Key Principles

E-mail, telephone, fax and voice are a few of the most common ways by which people can transmit a message. But they are not the only methods. In fact, there are an incredible number of ways by which a message can be transmitted to another person. While the pragmatics of every day life may seem to limit the usefulness of some of these methods, it is both interesting and important that employees understand that there are other alternatives.

For example, consider the telephone itself. In the past the transmission of a voice message was accomplished by stimulating electrons to move through a copper wire. But today far greater efficiencies can realized by transmitting voice messages as pulses of light over optical fiber cables. In earlier history written messages were hand delivered by couriers. But even this process was speeded by the Pony Express, railway system and then the airlines that moved great amounts of air mail. In the pre-electricity era more urgent messages were commonly sent in the form of codes that could be transmitted over line of sight distances in the form of smoke signals, pennants, semaphores and signal lights. As time passed, the telegraph, transatlantic cable and finally the "Marconi" replaced those methods.

Today, while we rely heavily on electronic means to transmit voice and data messages (satellite communication, cell phone and television being familiar methods), the written word, numerical symbols, pictures and other graphics seem to have survived as indispensable means for conveying encoded thoughts.
Whatever message transmission method is used, the key is to properly match the method with the message to ensure that the latter will be conveyed in the most effective, understandable way. This activity, though short in duration, will certainly help students to develop a better appreciation for that particular point.

The purpose of this section is to help you facilitate the activity effectively. Before administering the activity to your class or session participants, be sure to read it in its entirety. If there are any aspects of the Key Principles about which you are unclear we suggest that you review the subject by referring to one or more of the many reference works which are readily available at any public library and at most company libraries.

1. Introduce the activity by asking the class what method they used most recently to convey a message to another person. Ask them what other methods they use frequently. Turn the discussion to communication within your organization in general and ask the class what they believe the most common methods of transmitting (conveying) messages that the majority of employees and management use.

2. State the purpose and objective of the activity and then divide the class into teams of from four to six people each. Make sure that each team has the material required for the activity and then ask the teams to appoint a team recorder – a person who will write down the list that the team generates in its brainstorming activity.

3. Briefly review the purpose and principles of brainstorming. Then tell the teams that in five minutes they are to brainstorm as large a list as possible of the methods by which messages can be transmitted from one person to another or from one place to another. When they understand the assignment commence this part of the activity.

4. Halt this part of the activity after five minutes. You might ask the teams to count the items or ideas on their lists and to "lighten" things up by posting the counts so that a winning team can be determined.

5. Conduct a brief discussion about the various methods identified by the teams and relate their findings to all of those methods that really apply to your organization.

6.   Next, instruct the teams to select what they believe are the five most important ways to convey a message to someone else and ask them to list the kinds of message that each of the five methods is most suitable for transmitting. For example, the telephone is very suitable for conveying personal voice messages in which immediate feedback is desired by both parties. But, as most people have experienced, the telephone can also be used by telemarketers or political groups to convey one-way scripted messages, as well.

7.   Allow 10 minutes for this part of the activity. Once again ask the teams to report their findings and then discuss them. Be sure to relate the discussion to communication within your organization.

8.   After five minutes or so bring the discussion to a close. Ask for and answer any final questions and then adjourn the session.

```
┌─────────────────────────┐
│    Activity No. 5       │
│    Lots of Blocks       │
└─────────────────────────┘
```

Time: About 25 to 30 minutes

Purpose: The objective of this activity is to demonstrate to students that two-way communication is generally more effective than one-way communication.

Description: This is an activity in which students, acting as message senders, attempt to describe a geometric pattern to other students who act as message receivers. The design of the activity first simulates one-way communication with a total lack of feedback and then progresses through steps to full collaborative communication. The activity is fun, easy to use and very effective in demonstrating the weaknesses of one-way communication and the advantages of collaborative two-way communication with feedback.

Material/Props: Note pads with pencils or pens for all students and a flip chart with paper and marker. One copy of **Handout 5.1** will be required for each student who is assigned the role of message sender. As an option additional copies of **Handout 5.1** can be made available to all class members during activity debriefing.

Teams/Group: Optimum class size is from 12 to 24 students.

Application: Most suitable for employees at lower to middle organizational levels.

Ask almost anyone whether two-way communication is more effective than one- way communication and the response will likely be that it is. There has been enough discussion about the subject over the years that the question itself seems trite. However, the chances are that very few people can explain exactly why two- way communication is more effective than one-way communication nor, for that matter, can most people illustrate the differences between the two communication forms.

It is generally agreed that one of the least effective ways for someone to exchange a message with another person is to send a memo. This is because a memo is an almost perfect illustration of one-way communication. At the time that the memo is read the reader is at the mercy of the writer with respect to understanding the writer's intended message, the reasons for it and any response action that the writer may expect the reader to take. For example, consider the following e-mail message that one administrative assistant received:

> "Sarah, I am just boarding Flight 1256 to LA and will arrive there in about four hours. Call Harry and see if you can get him off my back. That whole Brisbane thing is really bugging me. Also, make sure that an update is ready for me to pick up when I get to LA. Lastly, make sure that my husband doesn't forget to pick up the kids after school today."

Well, hopefully a very effective Sarah will somehow be able to figure out exactly what Ellen wants done about Harry and the "Brisbane thing." She will also have to decide what kind of an update to send to Ellen where it should be sent so that Ellen can get it! Oh yes, what happens if Sarah can't get in touch with Ellen's husband? Even if she does reach him how is she supposed to make sure that he remembers to pick the kids up? Sarah would no doubt have liked to have Ellen clarify some of these issues, but as we all know cell phone usage is not permitted during a flight.

This brief anecdote illustrates the kinds of problems that often arise when communication is one-way – when the message receiver cannot respond with feedback or questions. Sarah needs a lot more information than Ellen provided in the e-mail in order for her to do a good job. But even the ability to exchange e-mail messages would not be as good as a person-to-person conversation in which Sarah could ask as many questions as she wanted and in which Ellen could receive feedback about how well Sarah understood her instructions.

The most effective form of communication is that which enables the message sender and receiver to respond to each other in a loop-like manner. The message sender communicates, the receiver responds indicating either understanding or the need for clarification, the sender clarifies or modifies the message and the receiver provides feedback about response action. This can be done effectively in person, over the telephone or live in a TV conference or in other ways that facilitate immediate or near immediate two-way communication. This activity demonstrates this point quite dramatically.

The purpose of this section is to help you facilitate the activity effectively. Before administering the activity to your class or session participants, be sure to read it in its entirety. If there are any aspects of the Key Principles about which you are unclear we suggest that you review the subject by referring to one or more of the many reference works which are readily available at any public library and at most company libraries.

1. Introduce the activity by asking the class to give you examples of what they consider to be the most effective and least effective ways to communicate with someone else. Choose a few responses from the class and write them on a flip chart. But, do not discuss them at this time. State the purpose and objective of the activity and tell the class that when they have completed the activity they will have a much better understanding about how they can improve the effectiveness of their method of communication.

2. Select four students from the class at random and assign them to pairs. Appoint one of each pair to be the message sender and the other to be the message receiver. Position each pair about 10 feet apart with their backs toward each other. The message receiver should have a flip chart available with the chart paper angled toward the class so that they can see what the person draws.

3. Instruct the class to make notes about the process that they will observe during the activity. Then give one copy of **Handout 5.1** to each of the message senders and follow the steps below:

    a. Instruct the message senders to describe the geometric pattern in **Handout 5.1** to their respective message receivers. Neither senders nor receivers are allowed to ask any questions of each other and senders are not allowed to look at the flip chart drawings of the receivers.

b. After five minutes tell the pairs that they may ask questions of each other but that they are to remain back to back with the senders unable to view the receivers' drawings.

c. After three or four more minutes tell the senders that they may now turn around and view the drawing of their respective receiver. They may now add this visual feedback to modify their verbal description of the geometric pattern.

d. After another three or four minutes allow the pairs to face each other and share mutual feedback but still at a 10 foot distance.

e. Finally, after another couple of minutes allow the senders to go to the receivers and help the receiver complete the pattern on the flip chart. Conclude by allowing the senders to show the receivers **Handout 5.1**.

4. Debrief the activity by first asking the class for their observations and comments. Then ask the senders and receivers for their comments, especially concerning the extent to which the accuracy of the receivers' drawings increased as two-way communication began to unfold. Conclude by pointing out that the quality and effectiveness of communication during the activity was at its optimum quality level when the pairs were working together collaboratively sharing all relevant information.

5. Bring the session to a close. Recap the main points brought out during the activity and ask for and answer any final questions. Then adjourn the session.

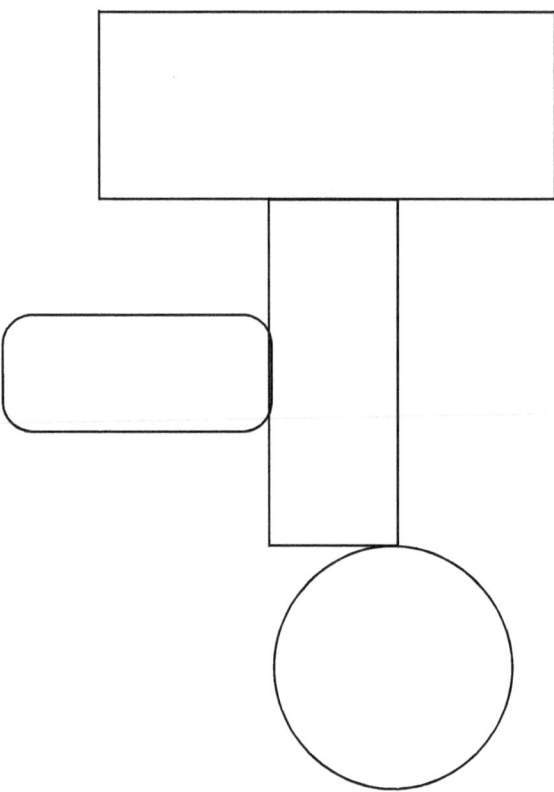

Activity No. 6
What I Meant to Say

Time: About 20 to 25 minutes

Purpose: The objective of this activity is to demonstrate that what we say is often easily misunderstood by others.

Description: Triads of students exchange examples of occasions when something they said was misunderstood or misinterpreted by another person. They then offer suggestions to each other about how the messages could have been phrased more accurately.

Material/Props: Note pads with pencils or pens, flip charts with paper and markers.

Teams/Group: Triads of employees in a class of 18 to 24 students.

Application: Most suitable for employees at lower and middle organizational levels.

Key Principles

Hardly a day goes by without each of us saying something that was interpreted by someone else in a way other than what we had intended. Most of the time the miscommunication is of little importance and after we obtain feedback that there was a misunderstanding we can quickly correct the problem. However, sometimes the problem is more serious and can result in hurt feelings, offenses being taken, business deals being lost and even international incidents created.

There is no guarantee that when we speak to someone else or when we write a memo or letter we will always be understood in the way that we had intended. However, it is an effort that we must make and one way to accomplish this is to think before we speak or write. A little caution beforehand will go a long way afterward. Still another way is to obtain feedback from the other person about whether or not he or she really understood your message.

Some of the feedback can be in the form of your observance of body language. Look for any signs of lack of comprehension, confusion, displeasure or offense (especially when you said something that you believe was non-offensive) or disagreement. Of course, you can always ask the other person questions to ascertain his or her understanding. But, avoid asking something like "Do you understand me?" That allows a "yes" or "no" response which may not be accurate. Instead, ask something like "How do you feel about what I said?" The latter type of question is more open-ended and generally better feedback than a close-ended question.

Remember, the bottom line is think before you speak or write and get feedback. How do you feel about that idea? (See, we practice what we preach!)

Facilitation Guidelines

The purpose of this section is to help you facilitate the activity effectively. Before administering the activity to your class or session participants, be sure to read it in its entirety. If there are any aspects of the Key Principles about which you are unclear we suggest that you review the subject by referring to one or more of the many reference works which are readily available at any public library and at most company libraries.

1. Introduce the activity by asking the class how often they have said something that was misunderstood by others. Select two or three volunteers at random and ask them to give examples including any negative consequences of the misunderstanding.

2. Inform the class that this will be a very short activity but that it will demonstrate that sometimes what we say is not what we mean and that it will help them avoid communication misunderstandings in the future.

3. Divide the class into triads (teams of three people each). Make sure that they have note pads and pencils or pens.

4. Instruct the individual members of the triads to write down one specific example of a situation when they said something that was misinterpreted by another person and when the misunderstanding caused a fairly serious problem or at least a serious inconvenience (personal or business). Allow five minutes for this part of the activity.

> Example: "I wanted to make a reservation for a double room for <u>next</u> Saturday. In this case the reservation was made on Monday with the intent that the hotel would book a reservation for the <u>following</u> Saturday. However, the desk clerk interpreted the word "next" to mean the Saturday of the week next after the current week. As a result there was no room available for me when I checked in to the hotel."

5.   At the end of five minutes halt this part of the activity. Tell the triads that each member of the triad in turn should now share his or her experience with the others and that in response the other members should offer their suggestions as to ways by which the misunderstanding could have been prevented. Allow 10 minutes for this part of the activity.

6.   After 10 minutes halt the activity. At random ask members of the various triads to present their examples and ask them to report what problems the misinterpretations caused. Then ask the other members of the speaker's triad how they believe that the speaker might have communicated the message so that a misunderstanding could have been avoided.

7.   Continue the discussion for a few minutes. Then, recap any important points you believe were brought out by the activity. Ask for and answer any questions and then adjourn the session.

Activity No. 7
Body Language

Time: About 25 to 30 minutes

Purpose: The objective of this activity is to familiarize students with the importance of body language in the process of communication.

Description: A facilitator led discussion about body language and its meaning leads to pantomimes by student volunteers and an interpretation of the gestures and expressions by the rest of the class. The class then views and interprets pictures that depict personages displaying body language in various forms.

Material/Props: Note pads with pencils or pens, flip charts with paper and markers, masking tape. **Handout 7.1**. Also, cut out and collect pictures from various magazines and periodicals of people interacting with others where clear illustrations of body language can be seen.

Teams/Group: This activity is designed for a class that consists of from 12 to 24 students.

Application: Most suitable for employees at lower and middle organizational levels.

Key Principles

Body language is the form of unspoken communication that takes place when one person observes the particular stance, gestures, facial expressions or other physical movements of another person's body, such as the angle that the person may be leaning in a chair or the tapping of fingers on a desk. It is an integral, unconscious part of our ability and skill to communicate with other people. Everyone uses body language. A mother scowls at a disobedient child and the child unconsciously reads or understands the mother's facial expression to mean displeasure or disapproval. Bored conference attendees yawn and shake their heads in a disapproving way. The alert speaker spots these body language signals in the audience and unconsciously responds by picking up the pace of the presentation. A postal clerk allows another customer to fill in a myriad of postal forms that should have been completed before the person got in line. Several other customers who are being held up show physical signs of impatience and annoyance which are easily read by anyone observing the delay.

All of these are examples of one of the most universal methods of communication known. Some studies show that when people are communicating with each other in person, well over 60% of the content of a message is transmitted via body language. There is no question that body language is not a game. It is an indispensable part of direct person-to-person communication and the ability of a person to *consciously* project and respond to body language signals can have a significant affect on their success on the job, as well as in their personal life.

Handout 7.1 provides several illustrations that show the meaning of various body language signals. None of the gestures or expressions in **Handout 7.1** will surprise you or the members of your class. But, there is one more aspect to consider about them. All body language gestures and expressions are made in the *context* of what is being said by one party or another. They must be interpreted in that context and sometimes the context is culturally specific. Body language senders, therefore, must be sensitive to any cultural nuances that their gestures or expressions might convey to people of another culture. This latter subject is beyond the scope of this activity but the reader should be aware that it is an important factor and he or she should take personal responsibility for investigating the issue further.

Facilitation Guidelines

The purpose of this section is to help you facilitate the activity effectively. Before administering the activity to your class or session participants, be sure to read it in its entirety. If there are any aspects of the Key Principles about which you are unclear we suggest that you review the subject by referring to one or more of the many reference works which are readily available at any public library and at most company libraries.

1. Introduce the activity by telling the class to look directly at the person who is seated to their immediate right, then at the person who is seated to their immediate left. Have them look at the other person's facial expressions, what they are doing with their hands and any other body movement signal that the other person conveys.

2. State that what people saw was likely a lot of laughter, people making funny gestures toward each other, maybe some people grimacing, others waving their hands around, and a great deal of other ways that people were clowning around. At the same time, add that the students may have noticed that some people looked ill at ease while still others may have looked annoyed that such a silly thing was being asked of them. But, explain in any case an incredible amount about body language can be learned from this simple illustration.

3. Explain what body language is and what it means. Distribute **Handout 7.1** to all members of the class and review the examples with them.

4. Ask for three to four volunteers from the class. Ask each volunteer in turn to stand in front of the class and perform an "off-the-cuff" pantomime using several body language gestures or expressions. Instruct the class to identify and interpret the meaning of each expression or gesture in the pantomime.

5. After a few minutes distribute the pictures that you have collected showing examples of body language. Again ask the class to identify and interpret the examples of body language. After five minutes bring the session to a close.

Handout 7.1   **Body Language Examples**

Body   *Meaning*
Language

Hands on hip, elbows out   Daring, defiance

Finger tapping   Boredom, impatience

Staring off into space   Mind is elsewhere

Hand pulling chin   Reflecting, thinking, evaluating

Fingers pressing nose   Repugnance

Arms crossed   Defensiveness

Palms of hands up or open   Openness

Hands clasped during negotiations   Withholding information

Foot on crossed leg pointed   Wants to leave
toward door

Furrowed brow   Puzzlement, worry

Wide open eyes   Surprise, amazement

Jingling coins in pocket   Concern about money

Foot on crossed leg   Nervousness
 rhythmically bouncing

Pursed lips   Anger, bitterness

Blank stare   Lack of comprehension

Hand rubbing forehead   Uncertainty

Activity No. 8
Context Counts

Time: About 20 to 25 minutes

Purpose: The objective of this activity is to familiarize students with the importance of context as it relates to the process of communication within the work environment.

Description: Students draw on their personal experience to develop a short list of examples of situations when the interpretation of a message they were sending was affected by context.

Material/Props: Note pads with pencils or pens, flip charts with paper and markers.

Teams/Group: This activity is suitable for a class of from 18 to 24 students.

Application: Most suitable for employees at lower and middle organizational levels.

Key Principles

Context helps to clarify meaning. It is the part of a verbal or non-verbal communication that gives specific meaning to the message being conveyed. We tend to think of context in a somewhat narrow sense, but from the perspective of holistic communication context is the totality of all of the circumstances that surround and encompass the transmission and receipt of messages, whether spoken or unspoken. For example, consider the following sentence:

"Well, here we go again. It's the last day of the month and I seriously doubt that Carla is going to get all the reports completed."

But, what did the speaker mean? Was it this:

"Well, here we go again. It's the last day of the month and I seriously doubt that Carla is going to get all the reports completed. That poor girl is so overworked it's a crime. She does the best that she can but there is just no way that she can handle that work load without extra help."

Or, was it this:

"Well, here we go again. It's the last day of the month and I seriously doubt that Carla is going to get all the reports completed. I tell you, she is the slowest person I have ever seen. How she keeps her job is beyond me."

Imagine that you are speaking with someone who is angry. In the North American culture it is usually fairly easy to see that the person, perhaps a customer, is dissatisfied. There is a usually scowl on the person's face and his or her brow is likely wrinkled and the lips might be pursed. We could also expect sharp, defensive and offensive words from someone who is angry. An angry man might stand with his legs a little farther apart than normal with his thumbs in his belt, signaling a somewhat threatening position. That certainly is part of context, but not all of it.

What were the circumstances that gave rise to the person's anger? Is this the fifth time that the customer has had the same billing problem? Was a sales person discourteous to the customer? Did the sales person say something that was overheard by other people in the store that embarrassed the customer? That is context. How is the person to whom the angry person is speaking reacting? Defensive, uncaring, arrogant, calm, helpful, apologetic? That is context, also.

How about the cultural background of the other person? In Latin American countries social relationships play a much greater role in the conduct of business than they do in the United States or Canada. The context of a prospective business deal in Mexico could well include a late and prolonged breakfast meeting and considerable time spent talking about each other's family. Business people in Mexico and much of Latin America invest a lot of time building a personal relationship with each other before either party would even think of discussing the business purpose of a meeting. Many foreign countries, like those in Mexico and Latin America, are "high context" countries. In contrast, the USA and Canada are relatively "low context" countries where people tend to be much more direct with each other.

Context also includes what is said and what is not said, how something is said, the body signals used to convey feelings or sentiments about what is said, and the same in reverse with respect to the person receiving the message. This can become very involved when you are communicating with people whose cultural background is different from your own. That is why it is important to develop a sensitivity to the issue of context in communication, which is exactly what this activity will help your students do.

Facilitation Guidelines

The purpose of this section is to help you facilitate the activity effectively. Before administering the activity to your class or session participants, be sure to read it in its entirety. If there are any aspects of the Key Principles about which you are unclear we suggest that you review the subject by referring to one or more of the many reference works which are readily available at any public library and at most company libraries.

1.   Introduce the activity by defining context and by presenting a brief overview of the subject based on the Key Principles for this activity. Call on two or three members of the class and ask them to volunteer examples of situations when they experienced a communication problem because of context. Discuss these examples briefly and then channel the focus of the discussion to the context of the work environment within your organization.

2.   Ask the class to think about the issue of context as it relates to communication within your organization. Mention things like people communicating with each other under stressful conditions such as when they face a deadline or when they are confronted with a quality or production problem. Then instruct each member of the class to write one example of a situation when the context of communication (either from them to others or from others to them) altered the message sender's intent and, consequently, caused a problem.

For example, in one company a supervisor of a certain work unit was under pressure to reduce costs. She was speaking to employees about the need for cost consciousness and made a comment that failure to cut costs could put the company in a difficult financial position. Some employees interpreted her comment as implying that a layoff was likely and began spreading that rumor throughout the whole company. No layoff was planned, the context of the supervisor's comment led employees to that erroneous conclusion.

3.   Use the above illustration to help direct the thinking of the class about their own job related context examples. Instruct them to proceed with the activity and allow 10 minutes before halting it.

4. Select members of the class at random and request that they state their example and explain it to the class. Briefly discuss each example and make notes on a flip chart in which you identify the context issue involved. Ask both the "volunteers" and the class in general how the particular context problem might have been avoided.

5. Select as many examples as your schedule allows. Discuss each accordingly. Be sure that you include intercultural communication context examples among those that you select and discuss. When you believe that the class understands the Key Principles of this activity bring the session to a close.

6. Ask for and answer any final questions and then adjourn the class.

```
┌─────────────────────────────┐
│      Activity No. 9         │
│      Do What?               │
└─────────────────────────────┘
```

Time: About 15 to 20 minutes

Purpose: The objective of this activity is to illustrate the need for
                    obtaining feedback when giving work instructions.

Description: A student roleplaying as a supervisor gives instructions to another
                    student who role plays as an employee. The instructions concern
                    placing and stacking several boxes. The instructions are given first
                    without the benefit of feedback from the employee. Next, a
                    modified version of the instructions are given but this time
                    allowing feedback. A comparison is then made concerning how
                    accurately the employee was able to follow instructions under the
                    two different set of conditions.

Material/Props: Note pads with pencils or pens, flip chart with paper and marker,
                    multi-colored markers and 8 boxes of various size of the type that
                    can be purchased at a commercial packing and mailing retail store.
                    Mark each box with a different letter of the alphabet. The first box
                    (regardless of size) should be marked "A" and the last of the eight
                    will be marked "H." **Handouts
                    9.1** and **9.2**.

Teams/Group: This activity is designed to be administered to the class as a whole.
                    However, at the facilitator's option it can be administered as a
                    team activity by dividing the class into teams of from 8 to 10
                    students each.

Application: Most suitable for employees at lower and middle organizational
                    levels.

The most important principle that applies to this activity is that a supervisor should always obtain feedback when giving work instructions to ensure that the employee has clearly understood the instruction. The principle is based on the truism that no employee can be expected to perform optimally unless he or she fully understands what is expected both qualitatively and quantitatively. In the first instance, the employee must have a clear, unambiguous understanding about the nature of the work to be performed and the method by which it is to be performed. In the second instance, the employee must fully understand the performance elements, like quantity, time or speed, and quality. Imprecise measurement terms like "too little," "not fast enough," or "not good enough" are unacceptable. Let's take a look at a couple of examples of mistakes of imprecision that supervisors sometimes make.

1. A warehouse supervisor gives instructions to an employee about storing certain material:

   "Mario, take that junk those guys from production dropped off and put it somewhere out of the way."

   What "junk" in particular? Where is an acceptable "somewhere out of the way?" When should Mario do it? Now? Next week?

2. A supervisor in a hotel is concerned that a night auditor is falling behind reviewing the day's receipts:

   "Andy, you're going to slow. Speed it up!"

   What is too slow, by how much should Andy speed up and to what specific level?

3. A customer relations supervisor is concerned about the way that an employee is interfacing with customers:

   "Felicia, you just must be nicer to these people."

What is it specifically that Felicia is doing or saying that the supervisor does not like? What is a standard for "nicer."

The above kind of communication from supervisors to employees is far more common than many people imagine. That is most unfortunate because it causes confusion on the part of an employee and frequently results in an improperly performed work task. In all three cases potential problems could easily have been precluded if the supervisor had simply obtained feedback from the employee about his or her understanding of the supervisor's comments. This short activity will dramatize the benefit of feedback in the process of giving work instructions and making work assignments.

Facilitation Guidelines

The purpose of this section is to help you facilitate the activity effectively. Before administering the activity to your class or session participants, be sure to read it in its entirety. If there are any aspects of the Key Principles about which you are unclear we suggest that you review the subject by referring to one or more of the many reference works which are readily available at any public library and at most company libraries.

Note: Before class begins place the eight boxes in the front of the classroom.

1. Introduce the activity by asking the class for examples of occasions when they were confused by the instructions that they received from a supervisor. Jot a few of these examples on a flip chart or marker board.

2. Present a brief (5 minute) overview of the Key Principles discussed above. Be as analytical as possible about the defects of imprecision in what the supervisor said in each example and on how the employee in each case might have interpreted the instructions or comments.

3. Ask the class how they might have avoided the problem if they were the supervisor in each case. Have them give examples of what they might have said to ensure greater precision in the instructions and how they might have obtained feedback from the employee to ensure that the employee understood the instructions or comments.

4. Now ask for two volunteers from the class. Appoint one to take the role of a supervisor and the other to take the role of an employee. Tell the person role playing the employee that he or she will receive instructions from the supervisor concerning the placement of the boxes and that he or she is to follow the instructions to the best of his or her ability. Add, however, that he or she will **not** be allowed to ask any questions of the supervisor or to make any comments about the instructions.

5.   Give the person role playing the supervisor **Handout 9.1**. Instruct that person to read the instructions contained in the handout aloud to the employee. Tell the supervisor that he or she is **not** allowed to ask any questions of the employee or to make any comment to the employee during the time that the employee is trying to follow the instructions.

      Note: At your option you can give copies of the two handouts to all members of the class so that they can follow along as the instructions are read by the supervisor.

6.   Allow no more than five minutes for this part of the activity and then call a pause. Ask the supervisor if the boxes are positioned as he or she instructed (highly unlikely). Now give the supervisor **Handout 9.2** and tell him or her to read the instructions that the handout contains aloud to the employee. However, this time tell the supervisor that after the instructions are read he or she should ask the employee to repeat the instructions. Also, allow the supervisor and employee to mutually clarify anything about the instructions that either party believes is necessary.

7.   Ask the class for the observations about the differences between the two skits. Focus the discussion on the extent to which the employee had difficulty following instructions in the first skit because of the one-way communication from the supervisor and the lack of feedback (response) from the employee. Then discuss the second skit and the extent that feedback and two-way communication helped the employee to more accurately carry out the instructions.

8.   After five minutes bring the discussion to a close. Ask for and answer any final questions and then adjourn the session.

Handout 9.1   **Instructions for Role Play #1**

As the supervisor in this role play activity you are to instruct the employee to place the boxes in a certain order and in certain positions. Do this by reading the following instructions:

> "I want you to place the boxes in an order from right to left. Place five boxes in a row: Boxes C, E, F, and H and A. Space the first four about one foot apart and the last one about three feet from H. Then place Box B in front of F and D in front of H. Stack Box G on top of E. Thank you."

Handout 9.2   **Instructions for Role Play #2**

As the supervisor in this role play activity you are to instruct the employee to place the boxes in a certain order and in certain positions. Do this by reading the following instructions:

> "I want you to first place the boxes in order of diminishing size from left to right. Space them one foot apart. Then Stack G on top of D, A on top of C and then place B in front of E. When you are done with that move the boxes closer together to the one foot separation I mentioned earlier to fill in the gaps left by the boxes you stacked on top of others. Thank you."

```
┌─────────────────────────────────┐
│        Activity No. 10          │
│          Listen Up!             │
└─────────────────────────────────┘
```

Time: About 45 to 50 minutes

Purpose: The objective of this activity is to demonstrate to students that the average person only retains a small percentage of what he or she hears in a conversation with another person.

Description: Teams of students compose short written stories that contain preassigned elements or events. They also prepare a short verbal test relating to the preassigned elements or events as they apply to their story. One representative from each team, in turn, reads his/her team story to the rest of the class. After each story is read the team representative administers the team's short verbal test to the class to determine how much of the story the class retained.

Material/Props: Note pads with pencils or pens for all students and a flip chart with paper and marker. You will also need up to eight copies each of **Handouts 10.1, 10.2 and 10.3**.

Teams/Group: This activity is designed to be administered to a class that has from 12 to 24 students.

Application: Most suitable for employees at lower to middle organizational levels.

Key Principles

Listening is one of the most important skills that you can have. How well you listen has a major impact on your job effectiveness and on the quality of your personal life. There are several reasons why we listen. We listen to obtain information that will enable us to do our jobs properly. We listen to understand our spouses, our children, other members of our family and our friends. We listen for enjoyment, like when we listen to music or when we watch TV or go to a movie. We listen to learn, whether we are attending a class in school or a special training class in the organization where we work.

In all of these examples, and many more, our listening effectiveness directly affects our ability to respond to what we hear in an accurate, appropriate and timely manner. But, here is the problem. It has been clinically proven that the listening effectiveness of the average person, before being trained in listening skills, is only 25%. Yes, that's right! Only 25%. This means that when the average person finishes having a 10 minute conversation with someone, like a boss, customer, friend or neighbor, he or she has understood and can respond accurately and appropriately to only 2.5 minutes worth of what was said. Imagine if the productivity of the average worker was that low!

Failure to listen effectively to others is one of the leading causes of misunderstanding and conflict. Poor listening skills result is more job related interpersonal problems that any other cause. The failure to listen to customers effectively results in more lost business than poor product quality, late deliveries and most other service quality deficiencies. Failure to listen effectively is perhaps the single leading cause of employee dissatisfaction in the work place. At home, poor listening skills can lead to strained family relationships, difficulties in raising children, conflict between spouses even divorce. Clearly, it is well worth the effort of everyone to develop improved listening skills as this activity will demonstrate.

The purpose of this section is to help you facilitate the activity effectively. Before administering the activity to your class or session participants, be sure to read it in its entirety. If there are any aspects of the Key Principles about which you are unclear we suggest that you review the subject by referring to one or more of the many reference works which are readily available at any public library and at most company libraries.

1. The most effective way to accomplish the objective of this activity is to launch into it without fanfare. In other words, demonstrate the Key Principles first and then discuss them. Therefore, begin the session by simply announcing that the purpose of the activity is to demonstrate how effectively the average person retains what he or she hears in a routine conversation with another person.

2. Next divide the class into three teams that, depending on total class size, should consist of from four to eight people each.

3. Distribute one copy of **Handout 10.1** to each member of the first team, one copy **Handout 10.2** to each member of the second team and one copy of **Handout 10.3** to each member of the third team.

4. Tell the teams that each of the handouts contains several core elements and events which can serve as the basis for a short story. Instruct the teams to compose a written story based on the information in their respective handout but not to exceed 200 words or a narration of five minutes in duration. Explain that each team will have the opportunity to tell its story to the other teams. Also instruct the teams to prepare a short verbal test that will determine the extent to which the members of the other teams (the listeners) effectively listened to and retained the core elements and events in their story. The test must be simple enough so that listeners can respond to it by writing responses on their note pads. Proceed with the activity and allow 15 to 20 minutes for the teams to perform these tasks.

5. After 15 minutes halt this part of the activity and ask a representative from one of the teams to read his or her team's story to the rest of the class. Tell the listening members of the class that they may not make any written notes about the story. Remind the story teller that the story must be told in not more than five minutes.

6. At the end of the five minute period instruct the story teller to administer the brief verbal test and similarly instruct the listeners to write their responses in their note pads -- individually and not as a team. When the test is completed have the story teller give the correct answers and allow the rest of the class to self-score their responses.

7. Determine a percentage score for each individual test respondent and use those figures as a demonstration of the listening effectiveness of the average person.

8. Continue the exercise by asking a representative from the second and then later the third team to read their stories, administer their tests, etc.

9. Conduct a short debriefing in which you focus on reasons why the class' listening effectiveness was not better. Draw out from them the extent to which they were hindered by listening barriers like lack of interest, distraction, prejudgement, prejudice, disagreement and others.

10. Bring the session to a close. Recap the main points brought out during the activity and ask for and answer any final questions. Then adjourn the session.

Compose a short story that contains any or all of the following elements:

- Four people named Beatrice, Agusto, Frank and Lynn, respectively.

- A picnic during the month of July at a park called "Silver Falls State Park."

- Picnic food consisting of potato salad, ham and cheese sandwiches, pickles, ice tea and cola and chocolate cake for desert.

- A chipmunk that wants food crumbs.

- Mounting clouds and a rain shower.

- Car keys locked in the car.

When you have completed the story prepare a test that you will administer verbally to determine how well others heard and understood your story. Include the above elements and the event in your test. Keep the questions simple. For example, you might ask: "During which month was the picnic held?" Or, "what food made up the picnic lunch?"

Compose a short story that contains any or all of the following elements:

- A meeting among a supervisor, Pat, and five subordinates, Inez, Terry, Carter, Mindy, and Susan, to solve a work problem.

- The meeting is held at 10:00 AM on Thursday in Conference Room B.

- Pat is concerned about a report showing that the work group's productivity rate for last month was 16% lower than the previous month.

- Terry and Carter seem to have a personal conflict brewing, Inez speaks English as a second language and has some difficulty understanding the problem. But, Mindy and Susan share your concern about it.

- The purpose of the meeting is to identify the exact problem and decide what facts must be gathered before the next meeting.

When you have completed the story prepare a test that you will administer verbally to determine how well others heard and understood your story. Include the above elements and the event in your test. Keep the questions simple. For example, you might ask: "Which employees seem to have a conflict with each other?" Or "Where was the meeting held?"

Compose a short story that contains any or all of the following elements:

- An auto accident that resulted in property damage but no injuries.

- The accident occurred at the intersection of Main St. and 7th Avenue South.

- One vehicle was a 1997 blue four-door sedan driven by a middle-aged woman. The other vehicle was a 2000 red SUV driven by a teenager.

- One of the cars ran a red light (you specify which one). The other was making a left turn from 7th Ave. South onto Main St. (turning from a southern direction toward the east on Main St.).

- One of the vehicles (you specify which one) struck the other a glancing blow (you specify at what point on the struck vehicle).

- Three witnesses saw the accident. The police arrived 4 minutes after the accident occurred. Traffic was tied up for 10 minutes.

When you have completed the story prepare a test that you will administer verbally to determine how well others heard and understood your story. Include the above elements and the event in your test. Keep the questions simple. For example, you might ask: "Who was driving the SUV?" Or, "At what intersection did the accident happen?"

Activity No. 11
Active Listening

Time: About 30 to 35 minutes

Purpose: The objective of this activity is to help students develop an
                   understanding about the principles of active listening.

Description: In this activity the facilitator takes the role of someone speaking to
                   another person and the class takes the role of the respondent. After
                   the facilitator verbally makes a statement or comment (reading from
                   a script) each member of the class indicates what he or she believes
                   would be an active listening response by checking off one of three
                   response alternatives in an answer sheet. Only one of the
                   alternative responses is an active listening response. A group
                   discussion based on responses to the facilitator's statements or
                   comments concludes the activity.

Material/Props: Note pads with pencils or pens for all students and a flip chart with
                   paper and marker. One copy of **Script 11.1** for facilitator use only
                   and one copy of **Handout 11.1** for each member of the class.

Teams/Group: This activity is designed to be administered to a class that has
                   from 12 to 24 students.

Application: Suitable for employees at all organizational levels.

Key Principles

Active Listening is the term that has been given to the one of the best ways to become a more effective listener. It means making a conscious effort to understand the total message being sent by the other person, listening to what is being said attentively, avoiding prejudgement and not allowing yourself to be distracted by what else may be going on around you and the speaker.

A second characteristic of active listening is acknowledging to the speaker that you hear and understand what is being said -- even if you do not agree with it. This can be done with a nod of the head or other body language or a verbal acknowledgment like "I see" or "I understand what you are saying."

There is still another critical element to active listening. Not only should you indicate to the other person that you are paying attention to what is being said, but also you must respond in a way that will both encourage the other person to continue speaking (conveying his or her <u>full</u> message to you) and also that will obtain the information from the other person you need to react in an appropriate way. For example, asking an occasional, non-defensive question for purposes of clarification or recapping what you understood the other person to have said in your own words, together with directly asking for further information, will clearly demonstrate active listening skills. Here are five steps that you can share with your students to help them improve their active listening effectiveness.

1. **Pay attention**. If you are engaged in one-on-one communication with someone look at him or her directly. Put aside distracting thoughts and try to avoid being distracted by noise or by whatever else may be going on around you. Pay close attention to the speaker's body language. "Listen" to that also. If you are part of a group or team do not engage in side conversations with others while one of the team members is speaking.

2. **Show understanding.** Indicate that you hear what the person is saying and that you are listening, even if you think that you might differ with the speaker's point of view. Show that you are listening by nodding or making other indications of acknowledgment. This will also help to make the speaker feel comfortable and it will encourage the speaker to express himself or herself more completely.

3. **Encourage dialogue.** Ask the speaker to provide you with more information and with a clarification of points that you may not understand. Do this by periodically recapping in your own words what you believe the speaker to have said and meant and by asking for clarification or additional information.

4. **Defer judgement.** Whether you like what the speaker is saying or not, wait until his or her facts and opinions are fully presented before expressing your own viewpoint. This means not interrupting the speaker with counter arguments midway in a sentence or thought that he or she may be making.

5. **Respond appropriately.** You gain nothing by attacking the speaker, putting him or her down or trying make yourself look superior. Be candid, open and honest in your response. There is nothing wrong with being assertive when you think that you are right. But in doing so treat the other person as you would like to be treated in a similar situation.

It takes a lot of concentration and determination to be an active listener. Old habits are hard to break and the chances are that your listening habits and those of your students are not much different from the listening habits of everyone else. But, it's not good enough to be just like everyone else especially when it comes to listening skills. That's why we designed this activity to help you help your students break those old habits.

Facilitation Guidelines

The purpose of this section is to help you facilitate the activity effectively. Before administering the activity to your class or session participants, be sure to read it in its entirety. If there are any aspects of the Key Principles about which you are unclear we suggest that you review the subject by referring to one or more of the many reference works which are readily available at any public library and at most company libraries.

1. Begin the activity by introducing the subject and by presenting a five minute overview of the process of active listening. Do this by first defining active listening and then by writing each of the five active listening step on a flip chart, briefly explaining each in turn.

2. Distribute one copy of **Handout 11.1** to all members of the class. Explain that you will act as someone who is speaking to another person and that in this activity each of them will be that other person. Tell them that after you make each of five statements or comments they will have 30 seconds to decide which of the three response alternatives in **Handout 11.1** would best illustrate an active listening response.

3. Answer any questions that the class may have and then proceed to read the five statements or comments in **Script 11.1**. Note that **Script 11.1** contains not only the five statements or comments but also the three response alternatives for each with the correct alternative printed in bold type. Pause after each item to allow time for the students to choose a response alternative.

4. After you have completed the above exercise begin a group critique in which you ask members of the class at random for their choice for each item. Then relate the correct answers with the five steps to achieve active listening that you presented earlier.

5. Recap the main points brought out during the activity and ask for and answer any final questions. Then adjourn the session.

Script 11.1   **Statements**

Note for Facilitator: Read each statement using the emotional tone suggested in italics. The correct active listening response is shown in bold type. The active listening principle relating to the response is shown in parenthesis at the end of the correct statement.

1.   *Read using a tone of annoyance:* "Oh, it's just the same old story, over and over and over again."

    a.   **Look at the speaker as though you are expecting him or her to continue**. (Pay attention)

    b.   Say something like "Yeah" or "Uh huh."

    c.   Take a note on a note pad.

2.   *Read using a somewhat angry tone:* "I know that most people disagree with me on this point but I think that we should shut the operation down right now!"

    a.   Voice your personal disagreement with that statement decisively.

    b.   Politely insist that the speaker justify his or her position on the matter.

    c.   **Say "I can understand how you feel about it."** (Show understand- ing)

3.   *Read using a frustrated tone:* "I don't know why we're wasting our time with this. She is going to do what she wants to do anyway."

    a.   **Say "You feel that she won't listen to our suggestions."** (Encour- age dialogue)

    b.   Say "I totally disagree. I think that she will listen to us."

    c.   Avoid conflict by remaining silent.

4.   *Read in a normal tone:* "I know it sounds crazy and in truth it may not be practical, but I think that we should redesign the whole project."

    a.   **Say "Well, why don't you give us your whole line of thinking about it?"** (Defer judgement)

    b.   Look at the speaker as though you are expecting him or her to continue.

c.	Smile politely.

5.	*Read in a slightly arrogant tone:* "Furthermore, I do not see how you could have possibly come to that conclusion. My own figures clearly show that sales in Region 7for last quarter are 5% above the previous period. I am sure that the others here will agree with me."

    a.	Smile and shake your head in disagreement.

    **b.	Say "I respect your disagreement but your figures are incorrect. Here is a copy of the sales report directly from Region 7."** (Respond appropriately)

    c.	Use body language to indicate your frustration at his or her obstinance.

Handout 11.1   **Active Listening Response Form**

Instructions: Below are five statements, each followed by three response alternatives. The activity facilitator will read each statement aloud using a certain emotional tone or inflection. After the facilitator reads each statement you will have 30 seconds to decide which of the three response alternatives best illustrates active listening. Indicate your decision by circling the letter that corresponds with the response of your choice.

1. "Oh, it's just the same old story, over and over and over again."

    a.   Look at the speaker as though you are expecting him or her to continue.
    b.   Say something like "Yeah" or "Uh huh."
    c.   Take a note on a note pad.

2   "I know that most people disagree with me on this point but I think that we should shut the operation down right now!"

    a.   Voice your personal disagreement with that statement decisively.
    b.   Politely insist that the speaker justify his or her position on the matter.
    c.   Say "I can understand how you feel about it."

3. "I don't know why we're wasting our time with this. She is going to do what she wants to do anyway."

    a.   Say "You feel that she won't listen to our suggestions."
    b.   Say "I totally disagree. I think that she will listen to us."
    c.   Avoid conflict by remaining silent.

4. "I know it sounds crazy and in truth it may not be practical, but I think that we should redesign the whole project."

    a.   Say "Well, why don't you give us your whole line of thinking about it?"

b.   Look at the speaker as though you are expecting him or her to continue.

c.   Smile politely.

5.   "Furthermore, I do not see how you could have possibly come to that conclusion. My own figures clearly show that sales in Region 7 for last quarter are 5% above the previous period. I am sure that the others here will agree with me."

a.   Smile and shake your head in disagreement.

b.   Say "I respect your disagreement but your figures are incorrect. Here is a copy of the sales report directly from Region 7."

c.   Use body language to indicate your frustration at his or her obstinance.

Activity No. 12
Be Nice!

Time: About 25 to 35 minutes

Purpose: The objective of this activity is to help students develop a
                     constructive interpersonal communication sensitivity that
                     demonstrates respect for the human dignity of others.

Description: Students are familiarized with both constructive and
                     unconstructive direct interpersonal communication. They gain
                     introspection and sensitivity by studying a sensitivity model and
                     by making lists of the kinds of constructive and unconstructive
                     things they believe that others might say about them. They are
                     then given the opportunity (strictly voluntary) of sharing their
                     lists with others in the class and of receiving feedback about their
                     self-analysis.

Material/Props: Note pads with pencils or pens for all students and flip charts
                     with paper, markers, and masking tape. You will also need once
                     copy of **Handout 12.1** for each member of the class.

Teams/Group: This activity will be most effective in a class that does not
                     exceed 25 people. Facilitators may conduct the activity
                     among the class in a general session or, if they choose, they
                     may divide the class into teams of from four to six people
                     each and conduct it as a team activity.

Application: Most suitable for employees at lower to middle
                     organizational levels.

Do you remember the children's jingle "sticks and stones can break my bones but words can never hurt me?" Well, it's not true. Words can hurt a person. In fact every day all over the world more people are hurt in one way or another by words than by any other single cause except, perhaps, by the ravages of extreme poverty. Whether deliberate or unintentional, communication insensitivity can be highly destructive. It can assail a person's dignity and sense of self-worth. It can demoralize, cause negative behavior like anger and violence, produce psychological and physical dysfunctions, and in the work place it can result in job dissatisfaction, low morale, low job performance and low productivity. Further, when people engage in insensitive and unconstructive communication they often find that there is a self-destructive backlash effect on them which can cause many of these same effects.

That's the bad news. The good news is that each one of us has the capacity to ensure that all of our personal communication with others is constructive – even when what we say is not what the other person would like to hear. In order to better understand this study the communication sensitivity model in Figure 12.1 below.

Unconstructive	Constructive
Untrue	True but Tough
Mean or Insincere	True and Positive

Figure 12.1

The labels in the four quadrants of the model are almost self-explanatory. But, let's take a moment to review them.

Unconstructive

Untrue: By any standard in any culture lying about people is wrong. Further, in certain circumstances lying verbally could be slanderous and doing so in writing could be libelous, both actionable in a court of law. Misleading or false comments about another person are the epitome of unconstructive communication.

Mean or Insincere: It is not constructive to speak disparagingly about other people whether directly to their face or, even worse, behind their back. Spreading word about someone's shortcomings, even if true, is called detraction and is morally wrong. It is also morally wrong to speak about someone in a mean, nasty or otherwise hurtful way. But insincere praise or flattery is equally unconstructive. Also, the transparency of insincerity usually reflects poorly on those who are insincere.

Constructive

True but Tough: No one is perfect. We all have weaknesses or areas where we can improve, whether they relate to our personal lives or how we perform at work. It is tough to receive criticism no matter how true or how justified. For a sensitive person it is equally tough to give criticism, no matter how constructive, to another person. The latter is one reason why research shows that only 10% of all performance appraisal interviews on the job are meaningful. The vast majority of managers and supervisors simply lack the skills to constructively coach employees about their performance. So, most just gloss over weaknesses or avoid talking about them entirely.

Still, most people want to know how they can improve themselves and respond positively to constructive criticism, whether given by a parent, spiritual advisor, teacher or work supervisor. The key is for the person offering the criticism to do so in a way that, while truthful and candid, preserves the human dignity of the other person and helps them improve.

True and Positive: Of course, this is the best of all. Perhaps another term for this is *recognition*. When we sincerely speak about a person's good qualities or accomplishments we give them recognition. This is true whether we compliment the person directly or whether we speak positively of them to others. By the way, this constructive behavior would be violated by omission – not speaking up in a true and positive manner when one should. For example, supervisors who fail to recognize the good work performance of employees are by their silence engaging in unconstructive communication!

The best way people can ensure that they communicate with others in a constructive way is to be sensitive about the possible consequences of their communication. As this activity will demonstrate all they really need to do is to think about how they would feel if they were spoken to or about in the same way that they intend to speak to or about another person.

Facilitation Guidelines

The purpose of this section is to help you facilitate the activity effectively. Before administering the activity to your class or session participants, be sure to read it in its entirety. If there are any aspects of the Key Principles about which you are unclear we suggest that you review the subject by referring to one or more of the many reference works which are readily available at any public library and at most company libraries.

1. Introduce the activity by asking the class if any among them has ever been offended by what someone else said, either about them to others or to them directly. Ask if anyone wishes to volunteer an example and if so choose two or three volunteers and have them respond.

2. Explain the purpose and objective of this activity to the class. Assure them that no one will be required to share private or embarrassing information with other members of the class.

3. Divide the class into teams of from four to six people each if you intend to make this a team activity. If not, tell the class that they will participate independently in the activity where they are seated. The process for either option is almost identical.

4. Distribute **Handout 12.1** to all members of the class. Read the instructions for each section of the handout aloud to the class. Then ask them to complete the form and allow 10 to 15 minutes for this exercise.

5. At the end of 10 to 15 minutes halt the exercise. Draw the model in **Figure 12.1** on a flip chart or marker board. Discuss the model with the class relating its Key Principles to the particular situation and circumstances within your organization.

6. Now ask the class how many of them found that what they listed as being hurtful or offensive for them would also be hurtful or offensive to others and how many found that what they perceived to be positive and constructive would likely be perceived as positive and constructive by

others. Ask if anyone would like to comment on their lists but do not require anyone to share that information.

7. Conclude by pointing out that being sensitive and constructive when communicating with others is a key to successful interpersonal relationships. State that underlying all of what was discussed and demonstrated in this activity is the timeless axiom "treat others as you would like them to treat you."

8. Bring the session to a close. Recap the main points brought out during the activity and ask for and answer any final questions. Then adjourn the session.

Handout 12.1   **Communication Sensitivity**
                              Checklist

In the space below make a list of some of the most hurtful, offensive or otherwise unconstructive things that others have said or that you believe they may have said about you. You will not be required to share this list with anyone.

_____ _____ _____ _____
_____ _____ _____ _____
_____ _____ _____ _____

_____ _____ _____ _____
_____ _____ _____ _____
_____ _____ _____ _____

When you have completed making your list circle those things that you believe would be seen as hurtful, offensive or otherwise unconstructive to others if said to or about them.

In the space below make a list of some of the most positive and constructive things that others have said or that they may have said about you. You will not be required to share this list with anyone.

_____ _____ _____ _____
_____ _____ _____ _____
_____ _____ _____ _____

_____ _____ _____ _____
_____ _____ _____ _____
_____ _____ _____ _____

When you have completed making your list circle those things that you believe would be seen as positive or constructive to others if said to or about them.

Now take a few moments to think about the overall quality of your communication practices with others. Think about how constructive your interpersonal communications are versus the occasions, unintended as they might be, when you tend to communicate with others in a way that may not be as positive and constructive as you would like. What can you do to improve the positive, constructive aspects of the way you communicate and how can you minimize the possibility that your communication would be seen as unconstructive?

Activity No. 13
Our Best Qualities

Time: About 45 to 60 minutes

Purpose: The objective of this activity is to help candidly deal with
                    diversity issues that impact intercultural communication.

Description: This activity takes the form of an intervention in which
                    interculturally mixed teams identify and discuss the best
                    qualities of each other's culture.

Material/Props: Note pads with pencils or pens for the teams, flip charts
                    with paper, markers and masking tape.

Teams/Group: Teams of four to six people each with a maximum of 25
                    people in the class. Additional facilitators will be required for
                    larger classes not to exceed 40 people in total.

Application: Suitable for employees at all organizational levels.

It is estimated that by the year 2005 over 60% of the work population in the United States will be comprised of women and cultural minorities. This shift can already be seen in almost every business, industrial and governmental organization at all organizational levels and in almost every job function.

However, while diversity is enriching our culture in many ways, it is also presenting new challenges. Not the least of these challenges concerns intercultural communication.

Living or working in a culturally diverse environment can be a very rewarding and personally enriching experience. It can also present many challenges to those in the diverse cultures. Many people feel strange or uncomfortable when they communicate with people who seem to be different from themselves. Sometimes the cause of this feeling is an unfounded bias or prejudice. Other times it can be based on a perplexing or possibly embarrassing past experience. In any event, if communication among people of culturally diverse backgrounds is not handled properly and sensitively it can result in unfortunate and unnecessary feelings of frustration and disappointment.

However, there are many things that you can do to improve your own intercultural communications skills and your personal sensitivity to the feelings, needs, fears and hopes of people of other cultural backgrounds. Here are four things that will make a big impact on how you relate with people of diverse cultural backgrounds.

1. **Develop empathy**. The single most important thing that you can do to improve the sensitivity and quality of your communication with people of other cultural backgrounds is to develop empathy with them. A major reason why each of us may have concern about someone who is different from us is because we do not know that person! Therefore, take the time to learn about the culture, customs, tradition, language and ethnicity of the person from another culture with whom you will interface. You will be amazed at the benefits that you will receive from gaining a view point from the other person's perspective.

2. **Confront your own prejudice**. We all have them. Maybe the fact that we have a prejudice is not our fault. Maybe we inherited the prejudice from our parents or society or from a difficult personal experience. However it was acquired, confront it honestly, rationally, recognize it for what it is and **get rid of it**!

3. **Look for signs of misunderstanding**. If you are a reasonably good observer of body language you will easily be able to pick up signs of misunderstanding on the part of your intercultural communication partner. Quietness, attempts to change the subject, inappropriate giggling, lack of interruptions, a somewhat vacant look and other similar signs are clear indications that your message is not being correctly received by the culturally diverse person. If you see any of these signs slow down, think about what you are doing or what you have said and try communicating with that person again.

4. **Respect the Values and Qualities of Other Cultures**. Every culture on this Earth is noble and therefore is worthy of respect. Here in America the peoples of all cultures are equal in the eyes of the law and as human beings we are all equal in the eyes of God. Every individual in every culture has intrinsic self-worth and dignity. Any reasoning person will be able to find values and qualities in any individual of any culture which are good, admirable and which should rightly command respect. One of the most important things that you can do if you really want to improve your relationships with people of other cultures is to look for the best in their values and personal qualities. That is a constructive approach that can quickly break down barriers that would otherwise inhibit positive intercultural relationships.

Facilitation Guidelines

The purpose of this section is to help you facilitate the activity effectively. Before administering the activity to your class or session participants be sure to read it in its entirety. If there are any aspects of the Key Principles about which you are unclear we suggest that you review the subject by referring to one or more of the many reference works which are readily available at any public library and at most company libraries.

1.   This activity is designed to be conducted among people of diverse cultural backgrounds. The value of the activity will be enhanced by having as much diversity as possible. For example, a class that had people of Native American, Asian, European, Latin and African descent or any similar mixture would be ideal.

2.   Introduce the activity by calling attention to the diversity within the class itself and within your organization. Present a brief lecturette based on the information in the Key Principles above.

3.   Divide the class into teams of from four to six people each. Construct each team so that the cultural diversity within the class is represented as best as possible. Make sure that each team is comfortably seated together and that they have the required material.

4.   Tell the teams that their assignment is to identify through consensus what the best, most admirable values and qualities are of the cultures represented in the class. Suggest that they first brainstorm a list for each culture represented and then refine the list through consensus decision making to arrive at the top 3-5 values and qualities of each. They are then to list these best values and qualities on flip chart paper and be prepared to explain their findings to the rest of the class. Inform the teams that they will have 20 minutes for this part of the activity and then tell them to begin.

5.   At the end of 20 minutes halt the activity. Ask the teams to post their findings on the walls near them using the masking tape provided. Then

call on a spokesperson from each team and ask each in turn to explain how their respective teams reached their particular conclusions.

6.   After all teams have reported their findings, conduct a debriefing discussion. Consolidate and summarize the conclusions of the various teams, which in most cases will likely be quite similar. Point out that this activity had several educational values. For example, it helped participants work together toward a common goal and thus helped to foster teamwork. In addition, intercultural communication and understanding was enhanced among team members as they gave serious thought to the identification of the best values and qualities of each other, explaining and discussing their respective view points as they proceeded with the activity.

7.   After 10 to15 minutes bring the discussion to a close. Ask for and answer any final questions and then adjourn the session.

Activity No. 14
Alien Language

Time: About 30 to 40 minutes

Purpose: The objective of this activity is to stimulate student thinking
                     about communication with people whose cultural
                     background may differ with their own.

Description: The scenario for this activity is a situation in which students
                     consider and discuss diversity communication by focusing
                     their attention on the variables that might be involved if they
                     were to attempt to communicate with a group of
                     extraterrestrial aliens who are visiting Earth.

Material/Props: Note pads with pencils or pens, flip charts with paper and
                     markers, masking tape. **Handout 14.1**.

Teams/Group: Teams of four to six people each with a maximum of 25
                     people in the class. Additional facilitators will be required for
                     larger classes not to exceed 40 people in total.

Application: Most suitable for employees at lower and middle
                     organizational levels.

Key Principles

This activity centers on how the students might communicate with a group of extraterrestrial aliens who are visiting the Earth for the first time. While the scenario might seem farfetched for some, there are others who might view it more liberally. Throughout history, mankind has speculated about our role in the universe. Millennium after millennium man would look out into the star- studded sky and wonder if he was unique and alone. Within the last few decades, however, we have entered into a new epoch that has allowed us to transform wonderment and speculation into scientific investigation.

Astronomers are now regularly reporting discoveries of planets orbiting suns in far off galaxies. It seems that life as we know it on Earth is the result of universal laws of chemistry and physics and many scientists opine that given the proper conditions and environment, this same process can occur elsewhere in the universe. For example, at a NASA sponsored workshop in 1975, it was concluded that given the origin of life elsewhere, cultural progress is a natural consequence of evolution under proper environmental circumstances, given enough time. In other words, if life itself exists on another world then there is a good probability that, with the right environment and conditions, intelligent life, followed by technology, will evolve.

A critical subject for investigation concerns the issue of establishing communication with extraterrestrials. There are many potential difficulties trying to communicate with a culture that may be unlike that of mankind in many respects. For example, it is obvious that people on Earth who have different cultural backgrounds may not understand one another. Imagine the potential for misunderstanding with communication between cultures that have much greater differences. The result could range from failure to understand an intended benefit to the cessation of contact.

In the scenario presented in **Handout 14.1** the students must realize that there would be major differences between an alien culture and terrestrial cultures, i.e. differences in history, traditions, customs, values, socio-economic systems, laws, religion, technology and much more, in addition to simple language differences. This understanding has very practical application at the work place, especially for multinational organizations or, for that matter, any organization in which people of different heritages and/or cultural backgrounds interact regularly. Meanings, semantics, verbal or written expressions, symbols and other components of communication not only might differ but very likely will differ among these people. The challenge, therefore, is to develop a greater inter-cultural sensitivity and awareness that can be made part of interpersonal and inter-organizational communication.

Facilitation Guidelines

The purpose of this section is to help you facilitate the activity effectively. Before administering the activity to your class or session participants, be sure to read it in its entirety. If there are any aspects of the Key Principles about which you are unclear we suggest that you review the subject by referring to one or more of the many reference works which are readily available at any public library and at most company libraries.

1.   Introduce the activity by asking how many among the class are science fiction fans. You might reference a couple of the better known science fiction movies like *Alien*, *Encounter of the Third Kind*, and *ET* and ask how many people have seen those films. Focus on the film *ET* (which most people will have likely seen) and state that although Hollywood seemed to have solved the problem of communicating with *ET* easily that might not be the case in a real life encounter with an alien.

2.   State that those who in the future may have to communicate with extraterrestrial beings may be able to anticipate the problems they might encounter by taking a look at the great diversity of cultures here on Earth, each differing from others in many and varied ways. Tell the class that this activity will give them the opportunity to gain a better awareness about intercultural communication and that it will do so by placing them in the roles of a special NASA task team.

3.   Divide the class into teams of from four to six people each. Make sure that the teams are comfortably seated and that they have the required material. Then distribute one copy of **Handout 14.1** to all member of the class.

4.   Read the handout aloud and ask the class to follow along silently. Make sure that the teams understand their assignment. Tell them that they will have 20 minutes to complete their discussion and that at the end of that time they will be asked to report their conclusions to the rest of the class. Begin the activity.

5.   At the end of 20 minutes halt the activity. Call on a spokesperson from each team and ask that person to briefly recap his or her team's findings. Ask the teams to relate their findings to the issue of diversity or intercultural communication in the work place.

6.   Briefly recap and summarize the findings of the teams, especially their comments about diversity and intercultural communication problems and sensitivities.

7.   Ask for and answer any questions that the class might have and then adjourn the session.

Handout 14.1   **The Aliens**

You and the other members of your team are to assume the roles of a group of communication specialists at the National Aeronautics and Space Administration (NASA). While NASA is best known for its role in the launching of the Space Shuttle and other space exploration projects, it also has had responsibility for a unique project called SETI, Search for Extraterrestrial Intelligence. SETI takes the form of radio telescope searches for signals from the galaxies which could possibly indicate that an extraterrestrial intelligence is attempting to communicate with Earth. However, a lesser known mission of SETI is to examine the issue of how humans could communicate with aliens from space whose cultural may (and very likely would) vary considerably from those among the people of Earth.

NASA has assigned your task team to serve as a "think tank" for the purpose of identifying and analyzing the considerations and variables that might confront humans in their first communication with extraterrestrials should aliens ever visit Earth. It has been suggested to your team that one way to go about this assignment is to reflect on communication among people of various culturally diverse backgrounds on Earth, especially in places where there is heavy intercultural interface such as in the work place, and to base your assessment, at least in part, on those intercultural communication problems.

NASA specifically wants your team to answer the following questions:

1.   What are the major kinds of cultural differences that might exist between mankind on Earth and extraterrestrial aliens?

2.   In what specific ways must humans be sensitive as they attempt to communicate with extraterrestrial aliens?

3.   What must humans consider with respect to the methods and forms of communications that would be used to communicate with extraterrestrial aliens?

```
┌─────────────────────────────┐
│      Activity No. 15        │
│      Survival Threats       │
└─────────────────────────────┘
```

Time: About 45 to 50 minutes

Purpose: The objective of this activity is to demonstrate the problem
                   solving benefits of collaborative information sharing.

Description: A list of conditions that could adversely affect a person's
                   chances for survival if lost is presented to activity participants.
                   The participants, first as individuals, identify and select the
                   seven most deadly threats to survival that a person faces when
                   lost in the wilderness from among those on the list. The
                   participants are then assigned to teams who must reach a
                   consensus decision about those same conditions. Post activity
                   debriefing focuses on the process and quality of information
                   sharing during team discussion including a comparison of
                   team scores versus individual scores.

Material/Props: Note pads with pencils or pens for the teams, flip charts with
                   paper and markers and one copy of **Handout 15.1** for all
                   participants.

Teams/Group: Teams of four to six people each with a maximum of 25
                   people in the class. Additional facilitators will be required for
                   larger classes not to exceed 40 people in total.

Application: Suitable for employees at all organizational levels.

Key Principles

Two-way communication is really the sharing and processing of information. There are many reasons why people share information with each other. Sometimes it is just for fun or entertainment, to socialize or to relieve boredom. But most of the time that information is shared within organizations the purpose is to provide a basis by which a decision can be made, including decisions that lead to problem solving.

Some will say that it is more effective and efficient if decisions are made and problems are solved by the brightest, most competent individual contributors in an organization rather than by group consensus. Indeed, many studies show that the brightest, most competent people in an organization can very often reach the "correct" decision in less time and with better quality results than the average team or group who is working on the same issue. So, it is not surprising that under certain organizational conditions it would be better to assign one person versus a whole team to make a particular decision. This could be appropriate, for example, when time was of the essence or when a particular individual had unique expertise related to a problem issue or when the acceptance of the decision by others was not a crucial factor.

However, for the past couple of decades there has been an increasing focus on team development in organizations and the realization that when all of a team's resources are effectively brought to bear on decision and problem issues the results can be spectacular! One of the major keys to this process is the extent to which team members fully participate in the communication and information sharing process that deals with the decision or problem issue.

But before teams can achieve their full decision making or problem solving potential they must be convinced that they can produce a result as a team that is at least equal to if not superior to what they might be able to produce as a collection of individual contributors. This is exactly what this short activity will demonstrate.

The purpose of this section is to help you facilitate the activity effectively. Before administering the activity to your class or session participants, be sure to read it in its entirety. If there are any aspects of the Key Principles about which you are unclear we suggest that you review the subject by referring to one or more of the many reference works which are readily available at any public library and at most company libraries.

1.   Introduce the activity by calling attention to the issue of teamwork within your organization. Lead a brief group discussion about the relationship between effective team decision making and problem solving and the quality of information sharing among team members. State that the purpose of this activity is to demonstrate that with full and effective information sharing among team members, the decision of the team as a whole can be as good as or even superior to the decisions of the best individuals on the team.

2.   Distribute **Handout 15.1** to all members of the class. Read the instruction portion of the handout aloud and tell the class that they have five minutes to check their selection in the "**Self**" column.

4.   At the end of five minutes halt the exercise and divide the class into teams of from four to six people each. Make sure that each team is comfortably seated together and that they have the required material or props including the copy of **Handout 15.1** which each person completed individually.

5.   Now instruct the teams that they are to reach a team consensus regarding which among the list are the seven major **Survival Threats** to survival that a person faces when lost in the wilderness. Tell them that you are aware that the situation is hypothetical. But, state that unlike the previous part of the exercise when they had to make a selection of conditions on their own, they will now have the benefit of sharing information among themselves as a team. The concept is that broader information sharing enhances the chances for a more accurate

decision – even if it takes longer to reach the decision as a team. Tell them that they are to check their team selections in the column marked "**Team.**" Allow them 15 minutes for this part of the activity.

6.   At the end of 15 minutes halt the exercise and read the correct answers to the class. Tell them that the correct answers are based on the findings of outdoor survival experts but do not allow yourself to be drawn into a discussion about why the correct answers are so. The rationale for the answer is not really relevant to the basic purpose of the activity.

7.   Score the exercise by arriving at an average individual score at each table, e.g., the sum of the number of correct for each person divided by the number of people on each team. Write those scores on a flip chart. Then, next to the average individual score for each team, write its team score. Identify any team scores which are better than their team's average individual score. Also, ask what the highest individual score was for each team and compare that figure to the team scores to determine if the team score actually beat the best individual score.

8.   Briefly present any observations that you have made about the quality of information sharing on the various teams, including the fullness of member participation. Draw out comments and observations from the class about this also.

9.   After about 10 minutes bring the discussion to a close. Ask for and answer any final questions and then adjourn the session.

Handout 15.1   **Survival Threats**

You are to imagine that you are alone and that you are lost deep in a wilderness area. The area is not arid but at the same time from where you are you cannot see any signs of running water. You are fully clothed in casual wear but you do not have extra outer clothing. The temperature at that time of year in the area varies considerably from day time highs to night time lows.
You have no special equipment with you – only what you would normally carry on your person.

Below is a list of conditions that could confront a person in your situation and which might threaten your survival. Some are potentially more deadly than others. Your task is to decide which among the list are the seven most deadly **Survival Threats** that could confront you. Check your selections first under the column marked "**Self**." Later you will have another chance to make a selection but then it will be as part of a team.

	Self	**Team**	**Conditions**
1.	____	____	Strength or Weakness
2.	____	____	Fatigue
3.	____	____	Age
4.	____	____	Hunger
5.	____	____	Pain & Injury
6.	____	____	Fear & Anxiety
7.	____	____	Health
8.	____	____	Boredom & Loneliness
9.	____	____	Anger & Impatience
10.	____	____	Thirst
11.	____	____	Cold & Heat
12.	____	____	Rain & Wind

Handout 15.2   **Answers for the Survival Threats**

You are to imagine that you are alone and that you are lost deep in a wilderness area. The area is not arid but at the same time from where you are you cannot see any signs of running water. You are fully clothed in casual wear but you do not have extra outer clothing. The temperature at that time of year in the area varies considerably from day time highs to night time lows.
You have no special equipment with you – only what you would normally carry on your person.

Below is a list of conditions that could confront a person in your situation and which might threaten your survival. Some are potentially more deadly than others. Your task is to decide which among the list are the seven most **deadly Survival Threats** that could confront you. Check your selections first under the column marked "**Self**." Later you will have another chance to make a selection but then it will be as part of a team.

	Self	Team	Conditions
1.	____	____	Strength or Weakness
2.	____	____	**Fatigue**
3.	____	____	Age
4.	____	____	Hunger
5.	____	____	**Pain & Injury**
6.	____	____	**Fear & Anxiety**
7.	____	____	Health
8.	____	____	**Boredom & Loneliness**
9.	____	____	**Anger & Impatience**
10.	____	____	**Thirst**
11.	____	____	**Cold & Heat**
12.	____	____	Rain & Wind

Activity No. 16
Telephone Courtesy

Time: About 20 to 30 minutes

Purpose: The objective of this activity is to increase students'
                       awareness about the importance of being courteous when
                       communicating with others over the telephone.

Description: This is a team activity in which students develop a list of
                       telephone communication practices which they believe are
                       discourteous to either the caller or recipient. After compiling
                       their list they decide how each discourtesy can be avoided by
                       employees in their organization.

Material/Props: Note pads with pencils or pens, flip chart with paper and
                       marker.

Teams/Group: Teams of from four to six people each with a maximum of 25
                       people in the class. Additional facilitators would be required
                       for larger classes not to exceed 40 people in total.

Application: Most suitable for employees at lower and middle
                       organizational levels.

In our modern business society the telephone is the second most common way to communicate with other people (the most common way is face-to-face communication). Telephones are everywhere and almost everyone has access to a telephone, especially now with the advent and proliferation of cell phones. While there are some underdeveloped areas of the world where telephone systems have not yet been fully modernized, conducting commerce across international boundaries by telephone is as common and easy as conducting business by telephone within a person's own hometown.

However, as is the case with any other form of communication, telephone communication has its pitfalls. Thanks to advanced technology including satellite communication, microwave cell phone systems and the use of optical fibers which are replacing copper wire telephone cables, it is rare that a telephone call cannot be placed or is interrupted because of systems problems. At the same time there is considerable room for improvement at the human factor level, particularly with respect to telephone courtesy.

Telephones tend to depersonalize communication. The very same people who would never think of being discourteous to someone with whom they are having a face-to-face conversation too often lose their manners when speaking with people over the telephone. It is a societal syndrom much like "road rage" in which otherwise nice people become demons when they drive a car. Below is some of the discourteous behavior that is commonly found when people communicate over the telephone. As you read the list consider that in 80% of the instances when people at work communicate over the telephone one of the parties is either an internal or external customer of the other party. Therefore, in the work place telephone courtesy is also an important customer service element.

Discourteous Telephone Practices

1.   Placing the telephone receiver on a desk instead of putting the call on hold. This can subject the caller to noise and background conversation.

2.	Poor transfer techniques. Callers hate being cut off for any reason but especially when their call is being transferred.

3.	Keeping a caller on "hold" too long. This is very discourteous and shows disrespect for the value of the other person's time.

4.	Addressing a stranger by his or her first name. Some callers, especially many who are older or who hold positions superior to the person answering the call, become very offended by this practice.

5.	Failure to promptly return a caller's message. It is true that one time management practice is to bunch telephone calls and return them at a set time of the day. But, common sense and the priority of a call should govern here.

6.	Unpleasant or annoyed voice. First impressions count! Imagine how customers feel when their call is answered by someone who conveys the image that he or she is annoyed by the call.

7.	Third party side conversations. It is not proper to interrupt your conversation with the caller to engage in a side conversation with a co-worker who wants "just a minute" of your time while you are on the phone.

8.	Speaking too close to or too far away from the telephone instrument. This can garble your speech or make it hard for the other party to understand you.

9.	Misusing the speaker phone or "squawk box." There is nothing wrong with putting someone on the speaker for conferencing or when it is necessary to keep your hands free, like when referring to papers or notes during the call. But, let the other party know that others can hear them in that situation.

Also, remember that the other party can hear you, and usually also people in the background, until the telephone connection is broken. Some people hear very unflattering things that are said about them from careless people who can't wait to complete a hang-up before venting their candor!

The telephone is a wonderful and indispensable communication tool. But, we all must remember that it is an extension of social intercourse with other people who deserve to be treated with the same consideration, respect and courtesy that they would be given in a face-to-face conversation. This activity will help to impress that point on your students.

The purpose of this section is to help you facilitate the activity effectively. Before administering the activity to your class or session participants, be sure to read it in its entirety. If there are any aspects of the Key Principles about which you are unclear we suggest that you review the subject by referring to one or more of the many reference works which are readily available at any public library and at most company libraries.

1. Introduce the activity by asking the class for examples of situations when they were treated with discourtesy over the telephone. Jot a few of these examples on a flip chart or marker board. Ask those responding what emotions they felt when they were the object of the discourtesies that they mentioned.

2. Briefly discuss the relationship of the use of telephone in business and the issue of customer service. Try to determine the extent to which members of the class believe that when they use the telephone at work they are doing so in the capacity of being the other party's internal or external customer or that the other party is their internal or external customer.

3. Divide the class into teams of from four to six people each. Make sure that each team is comfortably seated together and that they have the required material.

4. Assign the teams to brainstorm a list of telephone discourtesies. Tell them that they will five minutes for this part of the activity and then instruct them to proceed.

5. After five minutes halt the activity. Instruct the teams to select the five most serious (worst) telephone discourtesies from their lists and tell them that they are to decide what they personally can do to prevent each discourtesy from occurring in their work group in the future. Allow an additional five to 10 minutes for this part of the activity before halting.

6.   Ask a spokesperson from each team to report his or her team's findings. Make notes on a flip chart and discuss the main points as may be appropriate. When all teams have reported their findings consolidate the lists and the solutions and recap any consensus that you might observe.

7.   After a few minutes of discussion bring the session to a close. Ask for and answer any final questions and then adjourn the session.

Activity No. 17
Writing Memos

Time: About 30 to 40 minutes

Purpose: The objective of this activity is to help students improve the clarity of written memos.

Description: Triads of students write and then exchange a short business memo. Each member of the triad, in turn, critiques the memos of the other members.

Material/Props: Note pads with pencils or pens, flip charts with paper and markers, masking tape and a supply of red pencils or pens. **Handout 17.1**.

Teams/Group: Triads of employees in a class of 18 to 24 students.

Application: Most suitable for employees at lower and middle organizational levels.

Key Principles

Writing memos and letters is an inevitable part of conducting business. It is possible to develop a whole instructional unit about this subject and you might decide that is exactly what your employees need. But, for "starters" here is a short activity that is not so much about punctuation, spelling, or grammar as it is on clarity and simplicity.   In a nutshell, here are four common sense memo writing guidelines that will help your students do this.

1.   **Keep it simple**. Get to the point as quickly as possible. Avoid using jargon or "shop" talk that will not be understood by the message receiver. Don't try to be clever or sophisticated by using fancy words or unnecessary technical terminology. Say what you mean. Use as few words as possible without sacrificing content accuracy or clarity.

2.   **Be positive and constructive**. Remember that what you write can remain as a permanent record of how you express yourself to others. Also remember that what you write reflects on the person or organization paying your salary. Always be constructive and polite in your written communication. Try to be positive but do not sacrifice candor. There is nothing wrong with being politely assertive.

3.   **Anticipate the reader's reactions**. Just as you should think before you speak, you also should think before you write (or at least before you actually send the memo). Choose terms and expressions that will accurately convey your message to the reader and that can be accurately interpreted within the context of his or her environment and culture. Anticipate how the reader will react to what you write.

4.   **Invite further dialogue**. Keep the lines of communication open. Invite questions for purpose of clarification, ask for the reader's proposed solution to problems, and indicate your interest and willingness to listen to and consider the other person's point of view.

Facilitation Guidelines

The purpose of this section is to help you facilitate the activity effectively. Before administering the activity to your class or session participants, be sure to read it in its entirety. If there are any aspects of the Key Principles about which you are unclear we suggest that you review the subject by referring to one or more of the many reference works which are readily available at any public library and at most company libraries.

1.　Introduce the activity by asking the class how many business memos and letters they have received during the past year. Then ask them the extent to which they believe that those memos and letters lacked clarity or were written in a way that was unnecessarily complicated. The chances are that they will say that they have received many memos and letters and that many of them lacked clarity or were overly complicated.

2.　Explain the purpose of this activity to the class and then divide them into triads (teams of three people each).

3.　Distribute **Handout 17.1** to all members of the class and review it with them. Make sure that the class has the necessary materials and then tell them that they have 10 minutes to write a response to the complaining customer. Begin the activity.

4.　After 10 minutes halt the activity. Tell the triads to pass the memos that they have written to the person seated to their right. State that each triad member is to make suggested changes to the memo or letter that they are critiquing. Explain that the changes should be for the purpose of both clarity and simplification. Allow five minutes for this exercise.

5.　After five minutes pause the activity and once again tell the triads to pass the memo that they have been critiquing to the person seated to their right. Again instruct them to make suggested changes in that memo, the suggested changes of the previous triad member notwithstanding. Allow two to three minutes for this part of the activity.

6. When the set time has passed halt this part of the activity and instruct the triads to again pass the memos or letters to the person seated to their right. This will return the memo or letter to the original writer.

7. Now allow a few minutes for the triad members to review the changes suggested by their team mates and to discuss the suggestions with them.

8. At random call on members of the various triads and ask them to read the original form of the memo or letter and then to explain what changes were suggested. Ask the speakers how they feel about the suggested changes.

9. After you have surveyed the class and obtained a reasonable number of examples bring the discussion to a close. Ask for and answer any questions that the class might have and then adjourn the session.

Handout 17.1   **The Memo**

You are employed in the customer service department of the Heavenly Beauty Mattress company. Below is a complaint letter that you recently received from a customer. Your assignment is to write a reply memo to the customer consisting of no more than 100 words and that contains any or all of the following elements:

- unexpected production problems
- a shipping cost surcharge due to increased fuel prices
- the need to keep costs down in order to keep prices low
- yours is the best mattress in the market
- your company's excellent reputation
- your company's quality control process
- dedication to provide the best in customer service
- the warranty for the mattress purchased by the customer has expired

----

To: Customer Service Department, Heavenly Beauty Mattress Co. Dear

Customer Service Representative:

I bought your mattress almost three years ago and I haven't had a decent night's sleep since. It sags in the middle, the foam padding has compressed, I can feel the springs in my back and the side handles have torn off. When I complained to the store where I bought the mattress they told me that the warranty is the manufacturer's – not theirs.

I want you to take this piece of junk that is the opposite of heavenly and give me my money back.

Sincerely disgusted, Larry

Dorsalpain

Activity No. 18
Speaker's Bureau

Time: About 45 to 60 minutes

Purpose: The objective of this activity is to help students develop
                   skill in making oral presentations.

Description: The class is divided into teams which are allowed to select a
                   presentation subject from a list given to them by the
                   facilitator. As a team students prepare a five minute
                   presentation of their chosen subject, which is then presented
                   to all class members by the team member who picks the
                   "short straw."

Material/Props: Note pads with pencils or pens for all students and a flip
                   chart with paper and marker. Once copy of **Handout 18.1** for
                   each member of the class.

Teams/Group: This activity is designed to be administered to a class that
                   has from 12 to 20 students.

Application: Most suitable for employees at lower and middle
                   organizational levels.

Making a presentation before a group is very difficult for some people. In fact, for some it is more than they can endure – or at least so it seems to them. But today an increasing number of people in business and other types of organizations are required to stand before others and present their opinions, suggestions or findings. At work, for example, this might range from giving a sales or customer service report to higher management to explaining a work method improvement idea to fellow members of a continuous improvement team. At home it might involve voicing an opinion at a Parent-Teachers Association meeting or representing the views and concerns of a neighborhood group at a town council assembly.

Part of the discomfort some people feel when asked to make a presentation is caused by suddenly becoming the focus of attention. The adage that there is "safety in numbers" applies here. The same people who might feel very comfortable speaking up as a member of a large group or audience may very well develop a bad case of stage fright when they become the sole focus of attention as an information presenter. While even the most polished and experienced presenters have been known to feel pangs of panic when they speak before a group, there are methods and techniques that can help making presentations not only less onerous for many people but even a fun and rewarding experience.

Communication presentation is such an important subject that at some future time you might consider developing an entire course on the subject.
However, this short activity can be quite valuable as a way to develop student awareness about making presentations and for giving them few useful tips about ways by which they can improve their own presentation skills. Here are a few guidelines that will help you accomplish this.

Preparation

T *Know the Subject:* A solid understanding about the subject to be presented, whether it is statistical data about a product quality problem, a disagreement about a proposed organizational or operational change, or the advocacy of a political or social issue not only serves the

118

presenter as a base of confidence but also is crucial to the success of the presentation objective. Facts, examples, and other supporting data should be collected, understood and mastered so that the presenter is seen to have authoritative knowledge about the subject.

T   *Know the Audience:* It is not necessary to know all of the audience by name, though that would be fine, but it is essential to know as much as possible about them as it relates to the presentation subject. What is the audience's interest, background, opinions and knowledge as related to the presentation subject? To what extent is the perspective about the subject that the presenter will make either congruent with or contrary to the views of the audience. Does the audience know the presenter and if so what is their overall feelings about him or her as a person and as a presenter?

T   *Know the Setting:* The presenter should know what the physical environment of the presentation will be. This includes factors like facility size, seating arrangements, interior climate control, lighting, acoustics, and the availability of audio, visual and electronic presentation aids.

T   *Prepare Presentation Aids:* The quality of most presentations is greatly enhanced by the use of aids such as charts, graphs, video screen projections, handouts and similar aids. Also included here are presentation notes. The presenter should avoid preparing a script.
Instead, the main points of the presentation should be listed sequentially on index cards or on a notebook type computer that can be unobtrusively referenced during the presentation.

T   *Practice:* Practice may or may not make perfect. However, it most certainly will increase the chances that a presentation will be made smoothly and effectively. Practice will help identify any weak areas that need to be bolstered and it helps build presenter confidence and fluidity.

Presentation

T   *Address the Audience:* Depending on circumstances the presenter should very briefly introduce himself or herself, the subject and acknowledge the audience by thanking them for the presentation opportunity or by making some other appropriate acknowledgment. This would include acknowledging and thanking, if appropriate, the person who may have introduced the presenter and, again only if applicable, any notable personages in the audience.

T   *Present an Attention Getting Overview:* The audience should be given a good reason why they should pay close attention to the presenter during the presentation. One very effective way to do this is for the presenter to give a motivating overview of his or her presentation briefly hitting hard on any attention getting facts or data. The overview should also inform the audience about what exactly it is that the presenter wants to accomplish during the main body of the presentation.

T   *Be Articulate:* The presenter should speak clearly and pronounce all word correctly at a normal conversational speed (125 to 160 words per minute). Colloquialisms, slang and local jargon should generally be avoided unless understood by all of the audience and appropriate to the nature of the presentation.

T   *Maintain Eye Contact:* One of the downfalls of some speakers is that they tend to fixate their eyes toward the upper rear of the audience. Direct eye contact is essential for a good presentation and this means that the speaker or presenter should continuously (but slowly) move his or her head to establish eye contact with all parts of the audience.

T   *Convey the Message:* The presentation should cover all main points logically, sequentially, confidently and decisively. In other words, the presenter should get the intended message across to the audience as he or she practiced doing so.

T   *Recap and Conclude:* Overkill should be avoided. After the facts, assessments and considered opinions have been presented (supported, of course, by the presentation aids mentioned earlier) the presenter should bring the session to a conclusion. A recap of main points covered, final questions and answers, if appropriate, and an ending that calls for some type of action or follow up response on the part of the audience will usually accomplish this effectively.

The above guidelines are easy for most students to understand. Their understanding of the Key Principles will be enhanced, however, through the process of demonstration, which is the purpose of this activity.

Facilitation Guidelines

The purpose of this section is to help you facilitate the activity effectively. Before administering the activity to your class or session participants, be sure to read it in its entirety. If there are any aspects of the Key Principles about which you are unclear we suggest that you review the subject by referring to one or more of the many reference works which are readily available at any public library and at most company libraries.

1. Before class prepare a supply of straws for the lot which will be taken. Make sure that you have cut enough straws in half so that there will be one short straw for each team as well, of course, regular length straws.

2 Introduce the activity by asking the class how many of them have experience in public speaking, including making presentations before a group. Call on a couple or so of any respondents at random and ask them how they feel emotionally when they get up before a group to speak and also ask them to share with the class any tips that they may have about effective public speaking.

3. List the *Preparation* and *Presentation* techniques on a flip chart and conduct a brief group discussion. Focus on those Key Principles and any useful tips offered earlier by the respondents to your questions.

4. Inform the class that at least some of them will now have a chance to put into practice what you have been discussing by making short presentations to the class.

5. Divide the class into teams of from four to six people each. Distribute one copy of **Handout 18.1** to all team participants. Instruct the teams to make a consensus selection of one of the topics on the handout. Then tell them that as a team they have 15 minutes to prepare a five minute presentation of the subject which will be made by the team member who draws the short straw. Encourage the teams to use visual aids like listed points on a flip chart to help facilitate their presentation.

6. After 15 minutes take an appropriate number of the straws that you have prepared earlier (one of which is the short straw), go to each team and have the team members draw straws until one member on each team has drawn a short straw.

7. Use some chance or random method of choice to decide the presentation line-up among the teams. Instruct the first team's representative to make his or her presentation and proceed on to the other teams' presentations to the extent that your time schedule for this module permits.

8. After each presentation conduct a brief critique of the presenter's presentation techniques in which you focus on the quality of delivery in relation to any applicable Key Principles.

9. Bring the session to a close. Recap the main points brought out during the activity and ask for and answer any final questions. Then adjourn the session.

Handout 18.1   **Presentation Subjects**

Below is a list of presentation subjects. As a team select one of these subjects and together prepare a five minute presentation on that subject which you will make to the class. If none of the structured subjects work for your team then do not hesitate to use the last one suggested!!

1.   The perceived reputation of the organization's products or services in the industry.

2.   Effects of any recent organization changes.

3.   Opinions concerning organizational morale.

4.   Work improvement ideas.

5.   Recent events of interest in the community.

6.   Recent state, national or world events of general interest.

7.   Opinions about the current performance of the stock market.

8.   Ways to improve communication in your organization.

9.   The affect that e-mail usage has on your organization's computer network.

10.   Whether e-commerce is really a good thing.

11.   The best way to build teamwork in your organization.

12.   Whether "palm" type computers are really useful or necessary.

13.   Any other subject that your team mutually agrees would be suitable for the purpose of this activity's demonstration.

┌─────────────────────────┐
│   **Activity No. 19**   │
│   **Circles & Arrows** │
└─────────────────────────┘

Time: About 35 to 45 minutes

Purpose: The objective of this activity is to demonstrate how the flow of participation during a meeting or conference can be measured and evaluated.

Description: The facilitator instructs the class in the method of constructing a conference participation diagram which is used by observers to chart the flow and frequency of communication among members of a simulated business meeting. A post meeting critique is held to assess the results of the diagram and to help students understand the need for inclusion and active participation by all members of a meeting or conference.

Material/Props: Note pads with pencils or pens for all students and a flip chart with paper and marker. One copy of **Handout 19.1** for each member of the class. You will also need to arrange a conference table and seating for six people at the front of the classroom.

Teams/Group: This activity is designed to be administered to a class that has from 12 to 24 students.

Application: Suitable for employees at all organizational levels.

Key Principles

Conferences and meetings are common throughout business, industry and government. Almost all of us attend meetings of one type or another. Weekly staff meetings, briefing meetings, safety or grievance committee meetings, seminars, production meetings, town hall meetings, training sessions, family conferences, student conferences and many more types of meetings, large or small, are so common in our every day lives that we generally accept them as inevitable. The nature and purpose of meetings may vary but they all share one thing in common. People assemble for the purpose of processing and sharing information. And, yet, so many times this most fundamental purpose is not accomplished because of poor conference or meeting participation.

Meeting members should be expected to fully participate and to contribute to the accomplishment of the meeting's objectives to the extent that their ability will allow. This is very important to the success of the meeting and therefore all members who are participating should encourage the full inclusion of all other meeting members during discussion periods. The role of the participant is to participate; to ask questions, to share information (both facts and ideas), to offer suggestions, to disagree and to criticize constructively, and to encourage his or her fellow members to participate in a like manner. But often it is difficult for those who are in the meeting to objectively and accurately critique the quality of meeting participation. One way to do this is by using a conference participation diagram like the one shown in **Handout 19.1**.

A conference participation diagram is a graphic depiction of the communication flow that takes place during a meeting over a short periods of time. The diagram is prepared by observers who record the communication flow on flip charts or marker boards at randomly selected "cuts" of the meeting that are usually of five minutes duration each. It is easy to prepare the diagram. In **Handout 19.1**, circled letters of the alphabet represent meeting participants in the order in which they are seated at a conference table. For purpose of this illustration **"A"** is designated the meeting leader.

A solid line connecting two participants indicates direct communication from one person to the other. An arrow head shows the direction of communication (from one person to the person at whom the arrow is pointing). Arrow heads at both end of the solid line indicate that a response was made, i.e. two-way communication. Hash marks next to an arrow head show the frequency of communication from the other party to that person. For example, in **Handout 19.1 "A"** might have said "Thank you **"B"**, that is a good idea." That would be a direct communication from "**A**" to "**B**" and would be represented by a solid line between the two with an arrow head at "**B**'s" end and one hash mark next to the arrow head. Further, in the handout it can be seen that "**A**" spoke to "**D**" eight times and that "**D**" responded to "**A**" five times. Lastly, a dotted line to the center of the group represents an indirect communication from one person to the group as a whole. For example, "Well, how should we begin?" In the handout three indirect communications were made by "**A**" to the group in general. The diagram does not distinguish between statements and questions.

Now, refer again to **Handout 19.1.** In the five minute "cut" recorded by the observer it can be seen that the greatest amount of communication was between **A** and **D**. **B** and **C** seem to have engaged in a side conversation. **D** and **C** exchanged one communication each but **D** did not respond to **E**'s communication. **F** did not participate in the discussion at all. There were three indirect communication from "**A**" to the group in general, and so on.

The conference participation diagram is a very useful tool for assessing the extent of participation of members during a meeting or team discussion. It can be used as often as needed to help meeting participants develop a better process of inclusion among all members. You can easily demonstrate the benefits of this tool by conducting this activity as part of your communication skills training program and by encouraging the class to use the process whenever they want to critique the quality of the meetings that they attend.

Facilitation Guidelines

The purpose of this section is to help you facilitate the activity effectively. Before administering the activity to your class or session participants, be sure to read it in its entirety. If there are any aspects of the Key Principles about which you are unclear we suggest that you review the subject by referring to one or more of the many reference works which are readily available at any public library and at most company libraries.

1. Begin the activity by introducing the subject and relating it to the types of meetings held with your organization. Briefly discuss the extent to which the students believe that there is sufficient participation by all parties during the meetings that they attend.

2. Distribute one copy of **Handout 19.1** to all members of the class. Explain what a conference participation diagram is and how it works.

3. Ask for six volunteers from the class. Give them a simple topic to discuss, one that does not require any special preparation but about which almost anyone will have an opinion, i.e. a sports event, the economy, some recent organization or procedure change at your organization, etc.

4. Appoint a team leader and seat the volunteers at the conference table.

5. Appoint one or more observers and provide them with flip charts. Have them draw circles on the flip charts representing the seating of the volunteers at the table and ask them to write each volunteer's first name in the appropriate circle. Make sure that the observers understand how the diagram is to be drawn during the meeting "cut." Tell the observers to wait at least five minutes into the meeting before they begin to draw the diagram. The purpose of waiting is to allow the communication flow at the table to become more natural and relaxed.

6.   Tell the rest of the class that they may join in the activity by constructing their own diagram as they observe the conferees. Then begin the meeting and allow it to proceed for 15 to 20 minutes.

7.   At the end of 15 to 20 minutes halt the activity. Instruct the observers to tally the number of hash marks and to report the direction and flow of communication among the meeting participants.

8.   Briefly discuss the results of the conference participation diagram with the class. Call attention to any lack of participation or inclusion, any side conversations, and any conversations that dominated others with respect to frequency. Ask the class for their personal observations and any comments that they would like to make about the process.

9.   Recap the Key Principle of this activity and the main points brought out during the demonstration. Ask for and answer any final questions from the class and then adjourn the session.

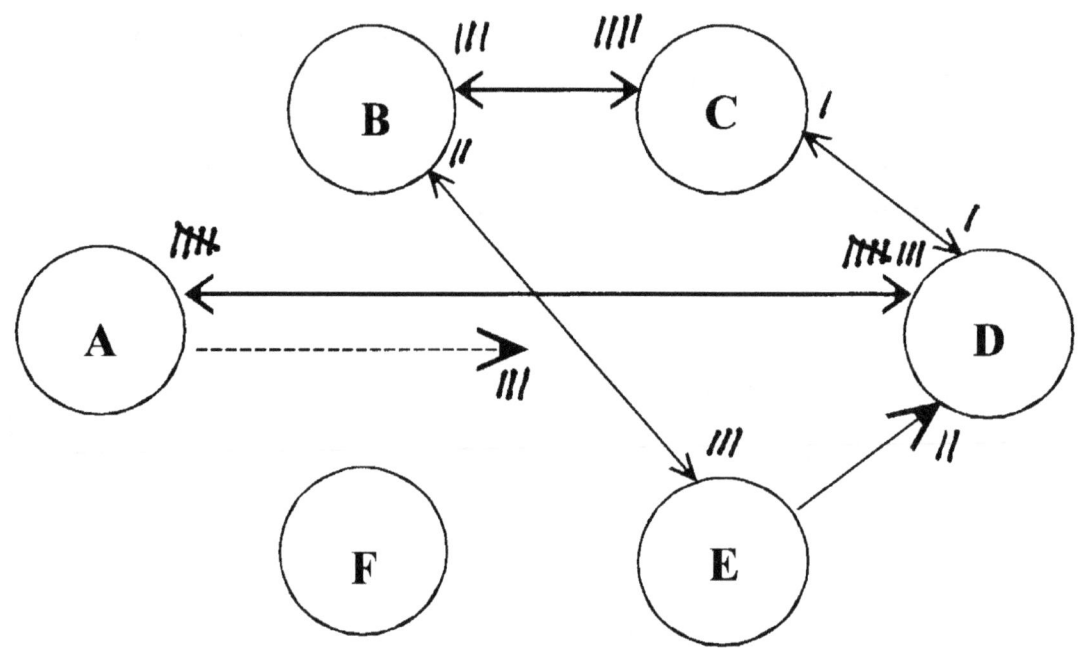

```
┌─────────────────────────────────┐
│        Activity No. 20          │
│        Coach the Coach          │
│                                 │
└─────────────────────────────────┘
```

Time: About 50 to 60 minutes

Purpose: The objective of this activity is to help students improve
                   their coaching interview skills.

Description: A facilitator led group discussion centers on the principles of
                   coaching with particular emphasis on the coaching interview.
                   Triads   of students then role play supervisor and
                   subordinate coaching vignettes.

Material/Props: Note pads with pencils or pens, flip charts with paper and
                   markers. **Handouts 20.1** through **20.3**.

Teams/Group: This activity is suitable for a class of from 18 to 24
                   students.

Application: Suitable for employees at all organizational levels.

Coaching is a companion skill to counseling. But unlike the latter, coaching always focuses on job performance. Coaching is usually initiated by a manager, supervisor or other work group leader rather than by an employee. During the coaching meeting or interview the focus is on the employee's job performance record. Opportunities for the employee to improve or to excel in his or her job performance are explored. Job performance deficiencies are openly and candidly confronted and discussed. In this way coaching is both evaluative and developmental.

Coaching employees in ways by which they can improve their job performance should be a regular part of a supervisor's planned work activities. It should be an on-going process consistent with the total quality management concept of continuous improvement. Unfortunately, studies show that only 10% of all managers and supervisors possess effective coaching skills. Still, with practice it is not difficult to improve one's ability to conduct a meaningful coaching session with an employee. Here are some guidelines that can help improve the quality of any coaching session:

1.   **Review the Purpose and Objectives of the Meeting**

Inform the employee that the purpose of the meeting is to review the employee's performance **record** in relation to job standards. Focusing on the employee's record (like on an attendance record or on a record that shows how many sales calls an employee made) helps remove subjectivity from the coaching interview process. Stress the developmental benefits that can accrue from the meeting and express your interest in using the meeting as an additional opportunity for both parties to discuss job related matters of mutual interest.

2.   **Ask the Employee for His or Her Self Appraisal**

Ask the employee to state his or her understanding about the performance standards for the job. Then ask the employee for a self- appraisal regarding how well those standards are being met. Use your listening skills. This is a good way to quickly promote a constructive discussion. The chances are that your subordinate will feel more comfortable and less threatened if he or she tells you how well his or her performance matched the work standard rather than have you do so. Studies have shown that in most cases when employees are asked for self appraisals they tend to be objective about the quality of their job performance -- even to the point of often being more critical than their superiors.

3.   **Seek Out Causes for Performance Variances**

If a performance deficiency exists it will not be corrected until both you and the employee identify the problem root cause. Only then will you be able to develop appropriate corrective action. However, you should be just as interested in learning what the employee is doing to achieve above average performance on any aspect of the job. That way you can help the employee identify behaviors that are contributing to success and possibly train other employees in these positive behaviors.

4.   **Inform the Employee of Your Own Assessment**

In the final analysis your own judgment, modified if appropriate by any new inputs from the employee, must be the governing factor. If you are using objective and documented job-related performance measurement criteria, then subject to the possibility of honest error your assessment must prevail. If the employee's self appraisal has not covered all of the issues completely or accurately, then you must do so now.

5.   **Develop Remedial Strategies**

Even when an employee has certain performance deficiencies it is likely that some parts of his or her job are being performed satisfactorily. Recognize any positive work behaviors and ask the employee what action he or she can take to correct performance deficiencies.

If the employee has no suggestion for ways to improve or if you do not believe that the suggested strategies will be effective then present your own performance improvement strategies for the employee. Set precise, measurable and realistic goals together a plan for accomplishing them.

6. **Discuss Additional Job-Related Subjects**

Take full advantage of this opportunity to discuss other job related matters of mutual interest or concern with the employee. Avoid "small talk" and non-job related, personal matters. Use this occasion to reinforce your ongoing willingness to listen to the employee and to be a coach, helper, and facilitator. Be sure to learn if the employee needs any special help or support from you in order to successfully accomplish the performance improvement objectives that were set.

7. **Summarize, Arrange for Follow-Up and Close**

Recap the main points covered during the meeting, including any action plans. Agree on what follow-up should be taken and when it will be done. Then, close the meeting on a friendly, positive note.

Coaching is a skill that requires considerable effort and practice in order to use it effectively. But it is a very crucial skill that all managers, supervisors and other work group leaders must acquire and regularly use.

The purpose of this section is to help you facilitate the activity effectively. Before administering the activity to your class or session participants, be sure to read it in its entirety. If there are any aspects of the Key Principles about which you are unclear we suggest that you review the subject by referring to one or more of the many reference works which are readily available at any public library and at most company libraries.

1. Introduce the activity by defining what is meant by coaching as it applies to the work environment. Point out that coaching always focuses on job performance. State that it involves both confronting employees about a performance problem and also coaching employees who are already performing satisfactorily in ways by which they can further improve their job performance.

2. Present a brief overview of the guidelines for coaching in the Key Principles for this activity, listing each one on a flip chart as you discuss it. Tell the class that the best way for them to truly understand the guidelines is to see them put into practice and that is why you will now conduct a role play exercise.

3. Divide the class into triads (teams of three employees each). Assign each member of the triad a role and give each person a copy of the appropriate handout. Also make sure that each triad has a supply of paper and pencils or pens. Ask them to take five minutes to read their respective roles.

4. After five minutes instruct the triads to begin the role play and allow the activity to proceed for 15 minutes.

5. After 15 minutes halt the activity and ask the observers to discuss their critiques with the other members of their triad. Encourage full discussion about the observations by all triad members.

6.   Allow the critiques and discussions to proceed for about 10 minutes and then halt the activity. Call on one or two triads and ask the observers to offer their critiques to the class in general. Encourage and lead any appropriate discussions. Be sure to ask how the supervisor in each triad handled the issue of the employee's excellent attendance record, about which the supervisor was likely unaware.

7.   After a few minutes bring the activity to a close. Recap the main points of the activity, ask for and answer any final questions and then adjourn the session.

Handout 20.1   **Role for the Supervisor**

Super Systems, Inc. is a high tech company that provides optical networking products and services. You (use your own name in this activity) are a supervisor in a department that handles the installation of the company's systems in customers' facilities. Your department has six technicians who are engaged in the installation of these systems. Every morning the technicians receive their assignment in the form of customer work orders. They then are supposed to go directly to the customer's facility, driving a company utility van that contains all required equipment and tools, and once there proceed with the installation. In most cases one technician can make two installations each day, one in the morning and one in the afternoon. Technicians maintain contact with your clerical assistant during the day via cell phone for purpose of making status reports, obtaining additional technical assistance and for similar purposes. All technicians are required to return to your facility and check out by the end of the work day, whether or not they have completed the last work order for the day.

You have been concerned about the job performance of one of your technicians (the person who is assigned the role of the employee). The technician has been employed in your department for two years. In your opinion that person's overall performance is barely satisfactory. You are particularly concerned with the following performance issues:

1.   From time to time he/she has been spotted by other technicians stopping for coffee and donuts while en route to a customer's facility. This is consistent with the fact that your clerical assistant receives 4-5 morning calls per month from customers who ask when the technician is scheduled to arrive to begin their installation.

2.   Two to three times per month the technician does not complete the afternoon installation and must go back to complete it the following morning. This causes scheduling problems for you and you believe that the problem may be caused by that person's late arrival at the first customer's facility in the morning.

3.   The technician's rework rate (occasions when he/she must go back to correct an installation problem) is 10% to 15% higher than that of the other technician's in your department.

Because of your concern you have scheduled a coaching meeting with the employee which is now about to begin. Your objective is to confront the employee with your concerns, find out what the problem is and develop a strategy that will improve the person's job performance.

Handout 20.2   **Role for Employee**

Super Systems, Inc. is a high tech company that provides optical networking products and services. You (use your own name in this activity) are a field technician in a department that handles the installation of the company's systems in customers' facilities. Your department has six technicians, including yourself, who are engaged in the installation of these systems.

Every morning you all receive your assignment in the form of customer work orders. You are then supposed to go directly to the customer's facility, driving a company utility van that contains all required equipment and tools, and once there proceed with the installation. In most cases one technician can make two installations each day, one in the morning and one in the afternoon. Technicians maintain contact with a clerical assistant in your supervisor's office during the day via cell phone for purpose of making status reports, obtaining additional technical assistance and for similar purposes. All technicians are required to return to your company's facility to check out by the end of the work day, whether or not they have completed the last work order for the day.

You are a single parent and it is tough getting the kids off to school before you go to work. Sometimes you are running so tight on time that you do not have time for breakfast. On these occasions you often stop to get coffee and a donut on your way to the facility of the first customer of the day. You know that you are not supposed to do this but you can't work on an empty stomach.

Otherwise, you are fairly satisfied with the quality of your own work. Nobody has complained about it and you get along really well with your customers. Also, you know that you have the best attendance record in the department. In fact, you keep your own attendance log and can prove it.

Your boss has scheduled a meeting to talk about your work. You wonder what's going on because he/she seemed quite satisfied at the time of your last performance review only three months ago.

Handout 20.3   Observer Checklist for Activity 20

Your role is to observe a performance coaching meeting that will be conducted by a supervisor in Super Systems, Inc., a high tech company that provides optical networking products and services. The supervisor oversees activities in a department that handles the installation of the company's systems in customers' facilities. The department has six technicians who are engaged in the installation of these systems. Every morning the technicians receive their assignment in the form of customer work orders. They then are supposed to go directly to the customer's facility, driving a company utility van that contains all required equipment and tools, and once there proceed with the installation. In most cases one technician can make two installations each day, one in the morning and one in the afternoon. Technicians maintain contact with a clerical assistant in the department during the day via cell phone for purpose of making status reports, obtaining additional technical assistance and for similar purposes. All technicians are required to return to the company's facility and check out by the end of the work day, whether or not they have completed the last work order for the day.

Your job is to pay close attention to the way that the supervisor conducts the coaching session and decide the extent to which he/she followed the performance coaching guidelines discussed by the activity facilitator at the beginning of the session. Those guidelines are listed below for your convenience. Make whatever notes you think are appropriate and be prepared to review your critique after the role play has been completed.

PERFORMANCE COACHING GUIDELINES

1. Review the Purpose and Objectives of the Meeting
2. Ask the Employee for His or Her Self Appraisal
3. Seek Out Causes for Performance Variances
4. Inform the Employee of Your Own Assessment
5. Develop Remedial Strategies
6. Discuss Additional Job-Related Subjects
7. Summarize, Arrange for Follow-Up and Close

Activity No. 21
Attitude Survey

Time:	About 35 to 40 minutes
Purpose:	The objective of this activity is to help students develop introspection about their personal communication practices.
Description:	This activity takes the form of a self-assessment of the students' personal communication practices. After completing the survey students are encouraged to develop their own strategies for improving any of their communication practices which are less effective than they would like them to be.
Material/Props:	Note pads with pencils or pens for all students and a flip chart with paper and marker. One copy of **Handout 21.1** for all members of the class.
Teams/Group:	Optimum class size is from 18 to 24 students.
Application:	Suitable for employees at all organizational levels.

Key Principles

This activity concludes the series in the compendium *Communication Icebreakers & Training Activities.* You might consider it to be the final practical application exercise. Because the survey covers a broad range of communication practices it also embodies essentially all of the Key Principles discussed in the other 20 activities this work. Therefore, you should review all of the Key Principles before administering the survey to the students and discussing it with them.

```
┌─────────────────────────────────────┐
│        Facilitation Guidelines       │
└─────────────────────────────────────┘
```

The purpose of this section is to help you facilitate the activity effectively. Before administering the activity to your class or session participants, be sure to read it in its entirety. If there are any aspects of the Key Principles about which you are unclear we suggest that you review the subject by referring to one or more of the many reference works which are readily available at any public library and at most company libraries.

4.   Introduce the activity by presenting a brief review of the major points brought out during your presentation of the other 20 activities in this series. You can use all of the Key Principles in this work together with any other reference reading that you may have done as the foundation for your review. Try to confine your review to about 15 minutes.

5.   Tell the class that the purpose of this activity, which they will complete individually and not in teams, is to help them reflect on their own communication practices, especially as those practices relate to the subject matter of the activities in this work. Explain that the activity will consist of a self-assessment survey and that no one will be asked to share his or her data with the other members of the class, nor will their assessments be turned in to you.

6.   Distribute **Handout 21.1** to all members of the class. Read the instructions aloud and answer any questions that the students may have. Point out that at the end of the assessment instrument there is an open- ended section where the students can summarize their strengths and development needs.

7.   State that the students will have 20 minutes to complete the assessment and then begin the activity.

8.   After 20 minutes have passed halt the activity. Urge the students to take their self-assessments home with them and to work out in their own fashion various strategies by which they can further capitalize on their communication strengths and at the same time improve those

communication skill areas where development is suggested. Offer to be available for counseling and coaching in the event that any of the students would like to take advantage of your communication expertise in the future.

9.   Bring the session to a close. Recap the main points brought out during the activity and ask for and answer any final questions. Then adjourn the session.

Handout 21.1   **Communication Practices Survey**

Instructions: Below are statements about common communication practices that could apply to any person. Read each statement carefully. Then indicate the extent to which you agree or disagree with each statement by writing one of the following codes in the appropriate column to the right of each statement: **SA**=Strongly Agree, **A**= Agree, **?**=Uncertain, **D**=Disagree, **SD**=Strongly Disagree. After you have responded to all of the statements read and follow the scoring instructions at the end of the questionnaire.

SA A U D SD

1.   The messages that I communicate to others are always clear and precise.

2.   I always make sure to obtain feedback when I communicate with others.

3.   My communication with others is always open and

4.   When I speak with others I am aware that there may be blocks that hinder the other person from my message.

5.   I seldom become distracted when listening to others.

6.   When listening to others I am always sensitive about any preconception or prejudice that I may have.

7.   I regularly practice "active listening."

8.   I use the most effective methods by which my messages can be conveyed to others.

9.   When making presentations before a group I often use aids like charts, graphs, pictures or handouts.

10.   When giving someone else an instruction I always ensure that I was understood by obtaining feedback.

11.   I have a good understanding about how to "read" body language.

12. When communicating with others I always consider the context within which my message will be interpreted by the other person.

13. Almost all of what I say to others can be characterized as being either True But tough or True And Positive.

14. Even when what I say is True But Tough I always try to speak in a way that shows respect for the other person.

15. I have made a point to become aware of cultural elements that can affect my communication with people whose culture may differ from my own.

16. When in a team meeting I try to include all of the other members in the team discussion.

17. I use only courteous practices when communicating by telephone.

18. When I write memos or letters I ensure that they are clear, to the point and that the grammar and punctuation is correct.

19. I have developed effective coaching and counseling skills.

20. I am fully satisfied with the overall quality of my personal communication practices.

Scoring: Give yourself 2 points for each Strongly Agree response, 1 point for each Agree response and 0 for any other type of response. Any single item that is less that 1 point and an overall score less that 30 suggests that you may need to work on your communication practices further.

Now, on a separate piece of paper list the five communication skill areas in which you believe you have the greatest strength and the five in which you believe you need the greatest further development. Take the list and this survey home. Make it a priority to develop strategies for improving your communication skill weaknesses and do not forget to continue to make full use of your communication skill strengths.

Appendix

Appendix A   Team Behavior Checklists

Team Process Observer Checklist

Use this form to record your observations about key behaviors that occurred during the exercise among diads, triads or among larger teams.

1. What was the title of the exercise and what was its primary purpose?

2. Did it seem that exercise participants understood the purpose and objectives of the exercise?

3. Did the participants establish and follow a rational process for solving the exercise problem or reaching a decision?

4. To what extent did the participants focus on the problem as opposed to going off on a tangent or engaging in behaviors not related to the problem or decision issue?

5. How well did the participants manage their time?

6. What is your assessment of the quality of interpersonal communication among participants during the exercise?

7. How full and active was the participation among team members? Was responsibility for problem solving/decision making shared by all or vested in only a few?

8. Did conflict or disagreement arise? If so, how was it resolved?

9. Did the participants reach a conclusion and solve the problem or otherwise resolve the decision issue? If so, how effective was it?

10. In your opinion how successful was the exercise as a learning tool?

Role Play Observer Checklist

Please use the format below as a guide to critique the performance of the principal player(s) in the role play exercise.

1.   Who were the principal players in the skit you observed and what were their roles?

2.   What were the main learning objectives of the role play?

3.   Overall how realistically did the participants act out their roles?

4.   Describe the key behaviors that you observed which were related to the learning objectives of this exercise.

5.   What were some of the expected and unexpected problems that arose?

6.   How well did the players handle any perceptual differences?

7.   List the most effective behaviors of the players during the role play.

8.   List the least effective behaviors of the players during the role play.

Team Leadership Observer Checklist

The purpose of this form is to critique leadership practices that were observed during the exercise.

1.   What was the title of the exercise and its primary purpose?

2.   Was there an appointed leader? If not, did leadership evolve naturally during the exercise?

3.   Overall, how effective was the leader in his/her leadership role?

4.   Describe how the leader guided the team to focus on the problem or decision issue.

5.   Describe how the leader guided the team to ensure that all team members actively participated in the team discussion.

6.   How did the leader handle any conflict situations?

7.   Was there any contest or competition for leadership? If so, describe what took place and how the leader handled it.

8.   How effective was the team leader's leadership style?

9.   How well did the leader help the team to accomplish its mission?

Session Critique Form

This form is to be completed by exercise participants in order to provide constructive feedback to the facilitator.

1. To what extent did you understand the purpose and objectives of the exercise?

2. Overall, how well were the learning objectives of the exercise accomplished?

3. Was the exercise fun?

4. How well prepared did the facilitator seem to be for the exercise?

5. Did the facilitator properly introduce the exercise and tie it I to the overall training program?

6. How effectively did the facilitator administer the exercise?

7. Did the facilitator conduct a meaningful debriefing after the exercise? If so, how effective was it?

8. How well will you be able to transfer principles learned from the exercise to real on-the-job situations.

9. Additional Comments:

www.ingramcontent.com/pod-product-compliance
Lightning Source LLC
Chambersburg PA
CBHW080250180526
45167CB00006B/2477